TABLE OF CONTENTS

INTRODUCTION

PURPOSE: This book on ANIMALS is designed to arouse interest in animals and encourage learning about animals. The book is designed with the express purpose of using an uncomplicated and direct format by which the student can become knowledgeable in science without the use of expensive equipment and costly laboratories.

The following activities vary in the length of time needed for completion so that they may be used in conjunction with other available materials. The scope of interest is sufficiently wide to enable the learning experiences to be many and varied.

How to use the activities in this book to the best advantage in your classroom is up to you. Please make the needed number of copies of each page.

ANIMAL ROTATION LAB

PURPOSE: To introduce the study of animals; to learn to observe the characteristics of animals.

MATERIALS: Gather up as great a variety as possible of living animals such as pet goldfish, frogs, insects, harmless snakes, pet mice, etc. Fill in with preserved specimens if they are available. To complete the lab, use pictures taken from old magazines such as *Ranger Rick*, *Wildlife*, and *National Geographic*. A metric ruler and information sheet are also needed.

PROCEDURE: Have students rotate stations at one to two-minute intervals and fill out information sheet for each animal or picture. An information sheet can be found on the following page.

ANIMAL ROTATION LAB

NAME	COLOR	SIZE	TYPE OF BODY COVERING	BACKBONE		TYPE OF APPENDAGES
				YES	NO	

CLAY PROTOZOA

PURPOSE: To acquaint student with the structures found in three types of protozoa: amoeba, paramecium, and euglena. This lab is also designed to show students that protozoans are not flat as they appear to be in pictures and under the microscope.

MATERIALS: Clay, broom bristles, and string

PROCEDURE: During or after the study of protozoa, the students will form the shapes of an amoeba, paramecium, and euglena. The string is used for making the whip or flagella on the euglena, and the broom bristles for the cilia on the paramecium. The important thing in the making of these protozoans is that they are not flat. The amoeba should be three dimensional with false feet (or pseudopodia) extending upwards as well as below. Euglena and paramecium are not flat, but are more or less cigar-shaped. The main features of these protozoans can be put in with the hands or the use of a pencil.

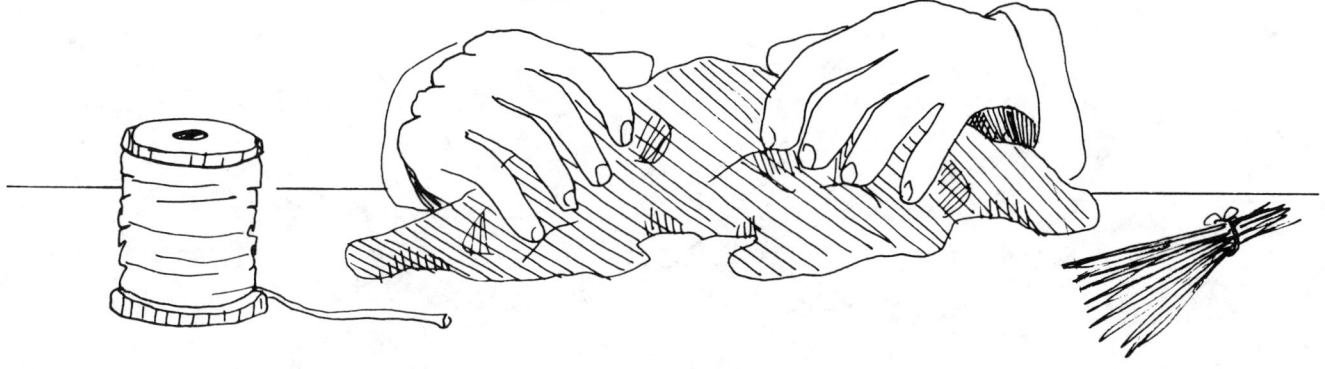

Clay Protozoa

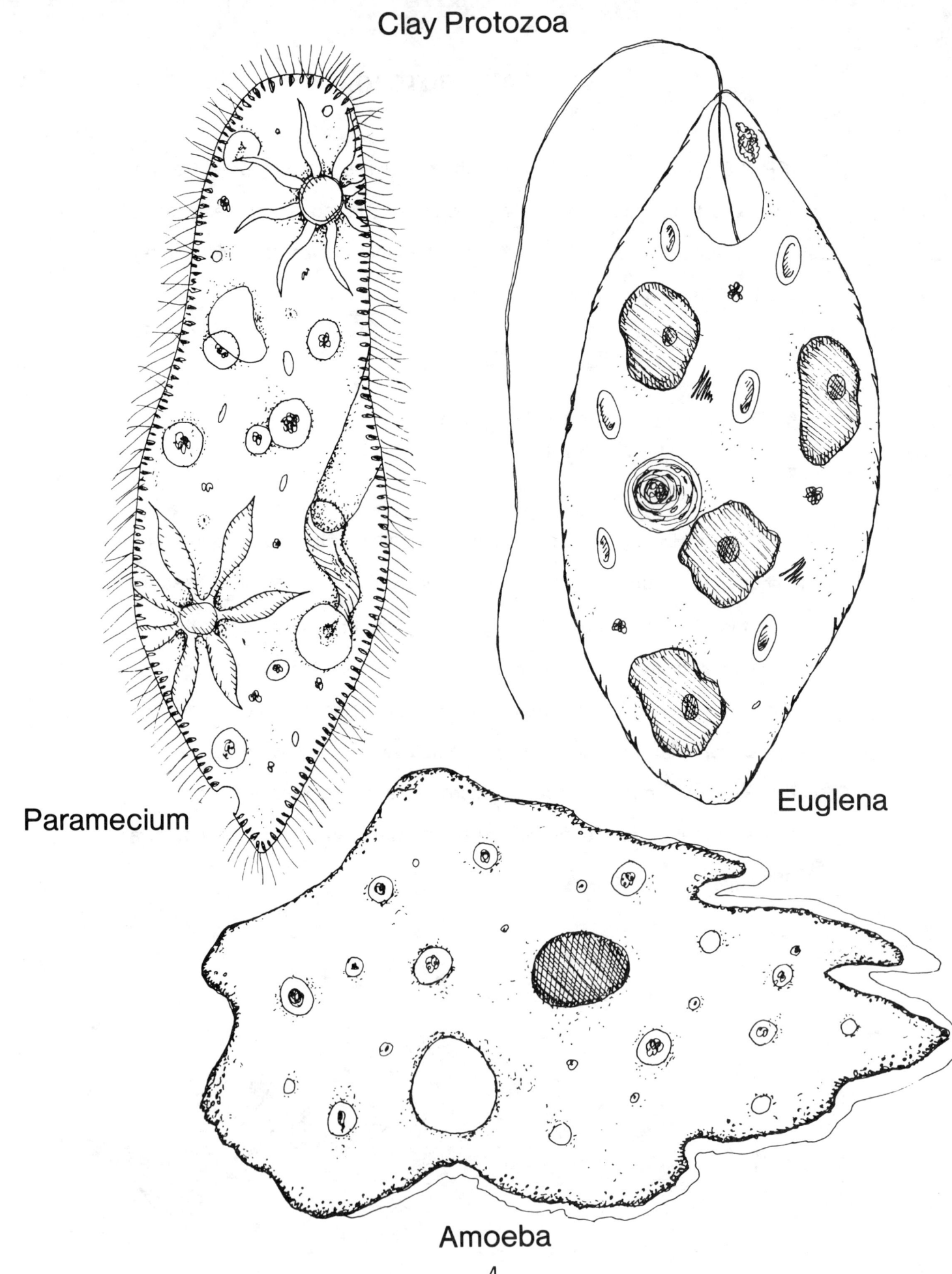

Paramecium

Euglena

Amoeba

4

WORM KEY

PURPOSE: To give students practice in using a key; to add interest to the study of worms.

MATERIALS: Live or preserved specimens, pictures or drawings as provided on the next page

PROCEDURE: A key is a valuable tool to anyone interested in the identification of living things. In using a key a student takes all the information he knows about an object and follows the given steps. In order to find the name of the worms, determine if the description 1A or 1B fits, then follow as directed. For example, in the key below, 1A tells the student to "See 2."

1A	Body round	See 2
1B	Body flat	See 5
2A	Body round without segments	Ascaris
2B	Body round with segments	See 3
3A	Body short, round, and segmented	Leech
3B	Body long, round, and segmented	See 4
4A	Clitellum present, no visible mouthparts	Earthworm
4B	Clitellum absent, mouthparts visible	Sandworm
5A	Body short, eye spots visible	Planaria
5B	Body long and ribbon-like hooks and suckers visible	Tapeworm

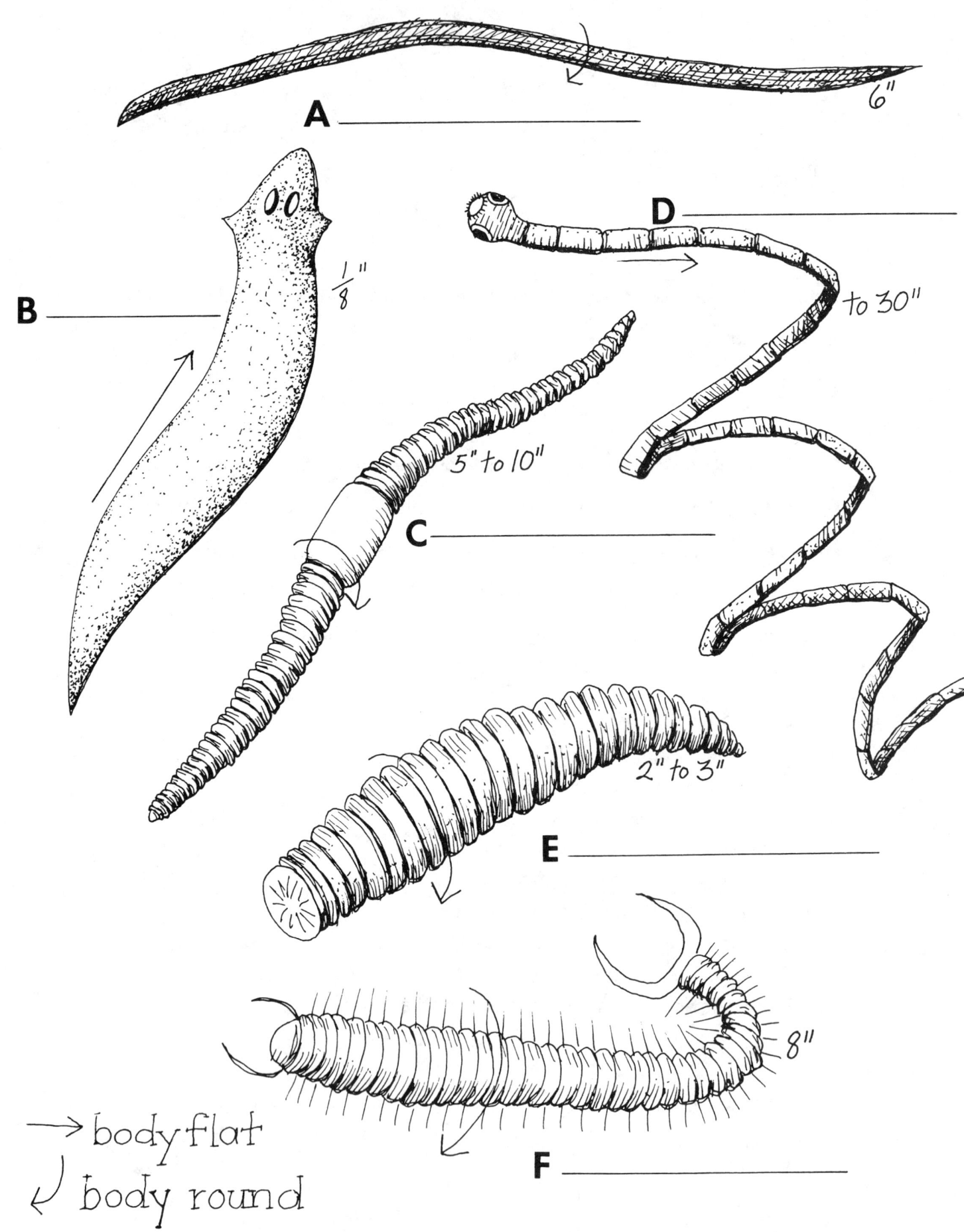

A _____ 6"

B _____ $\frac{1}{8}$"

D _____ to 30"

C _____ 5" to 10"

E _____ 2" to 3"

F _____ 8"

→ body flat

↳ body round

LIVE EARTHWORM LAB

PURPOSE: This is an observation lab on the behavior and external features of the earthworm.

MATERIALS: Live earthworms, hand lens, damp paper toweling

PROCEDURE: For each student or pair of students, an earthworm is placed on damp paper toweling. The student studies the earthworm and then proceeds with the following questions:

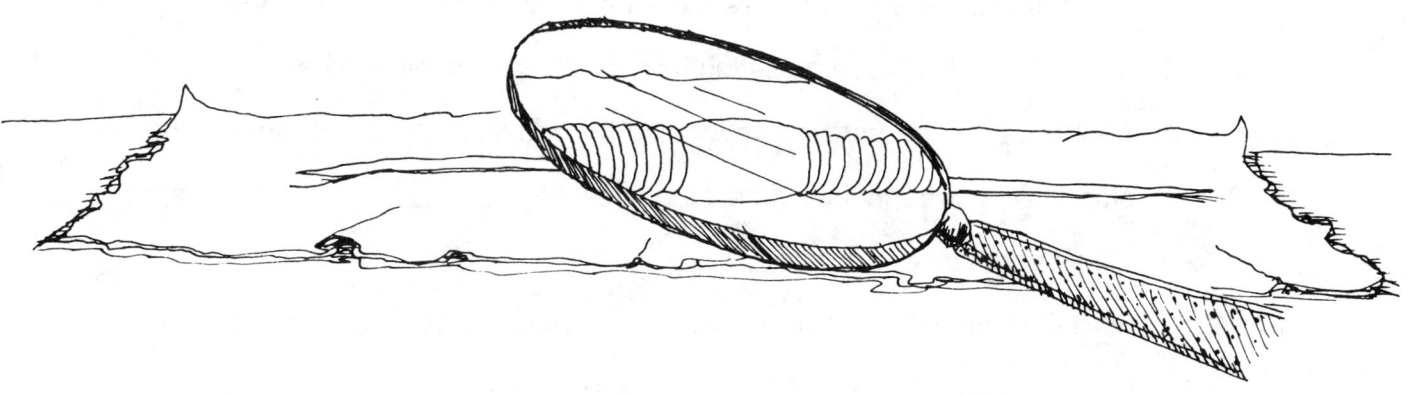

1. Watch the earthworm for one minute; then record your first reactions to it. _____
    _____
    _____
    _____

2. Describe how the earthworm appears to move. _____
    _____
    _____

3. Does watching the earthworm move help you to determine the head and the tail ends? _____

7

LIVE EARTHWORM LAB (cont'd.)

4. What is the shape of the head end? _____

_____

5. What is the shape of the tail end? _____

_____

6. Examine with a hand lens, if available, the top and bottom sides. Feel

both sides for bristle-like parts (setae).

7. Where are the setae located? _____

_____

8. How does the earthworm use its setae?_____

_____

_____

9. Try to find a large blood vessel on the back (dorsal) side of its body.

10. Can you see the blood pulsating through the dorsal blood vessel?_____

11. Can you take the earthworm's pulse by counting the pulsations as the

blood flows through the dorsal blood vessels? _____

12. Count your pulse. _____

13. Find the upper lip and light-colored band on the earthworm's body.

14. Can you count the segments in your specimen? _____

_____

15. What words describe the behavior of this segmented worm? _____

_____

16. Circle the body systems which you determined the earthworm to have.

a. circulatory   b. skeletal   c. excretory

d. nervous   e. digestive   f. muscular

g. reproductive

SYMMETRY

PURPOSE: In the study of living things the body plan or symmetry of an organism is important. The words *bilaterally* and *radially symmetrical* are often used descriptively in the texts, especially during the study of Echinoderms. It is to give students a better understanding of these terms that this exercise is directed.

MATERIALS: This exercise can be done in various ways. Objects can be used such as toy cars, airplanes, buttons, wheels, checkers, eating utensils, cups, saucers, etc. Attractively mounted pictures of objects can be used in place of the objects or in conjunction with the objects. A third suggestion is a ditto sheet with drawings (see sample next page).

PROCEDURE: If the teacher chooses to use objects, she can either gather one set for the class or make up several sets in sacks for teamwork or as a learning station. Small toys of objects and animals work well. The students look at the objects and decide the body plan or symmetry. Pictures are used in the same way. When ditto sheets are used, the students fill them out according to directions.

 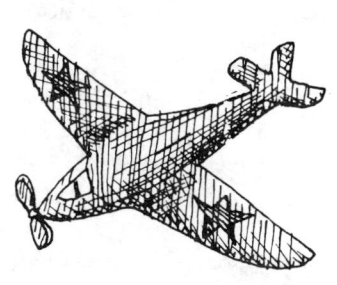 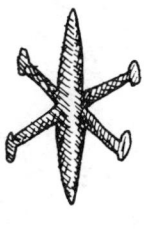 

SYMMETRY

Give the symmetry, either bilateral or radial, of the animals below:

1. Whale

2. Frog

3. Snake

4. Bat

5. Sand Dollar

6. Dragonfly

7. Walrus

8. Starfish

9. Goose

10. Fly

11. Brittle Star

12. Sea Urchin

1. Whale	____	7. Walrus	____
2. Frog	____	8. Starfish	____
3. Snake	____	9. Goose	____
4. Bat	____	10. Fly	____
5. Sand Dollar	____	11. Brittle Star	____
6. Dragonfly	____	12. Sea Urchin	____

SYMMETRY

Most animals have a front end, the end of the body that points in the direction of movement. This is the **anterior end**. The opposite end, that is the part that trails along, is the **posterior end**. If we divide such an animal, we have right and left sides that are very much alike. This kind of body design is called **bilateral symmetry** (as is found in man). Many echinoderms, such as the starfish have a different kind of symmetry. You can see that a starfish has no right or left sides, no anterior or posterior ends. There are many ways you can cut through a starfish and get approximately equal parts (like a pizza pie). This body design is called **radial symmetry**, because parts radiate from a center, as spokes from the hub of a wheel.

ACTIVITY: Place the ten objects before you in alphabetical order. Study each object and determine whether its design is bilaterally or radially symmetrical.

OBJECT	BILATERALLY SYMMETRICAL	RADIALLY SYMMETRICAL
1.		
2.		
3.		
4.		
5.		
6.		
7.		
8.		
9.		
10.		

INSECT ROTATION LAB

PURPOSE: To arouse interest in the study of insects, to identify their parts, and to become aware of their relationship to man.

MATERIALS: During the fall of the year, the spring, or perhaps during a field trip, assign students the task of bringing in five insects in as perfect condition as possible. From this group of insects, select a variety for stations in a rotation lab.

PROCEDURE: Have students rotate stations and fill out the information sheet. (Example on the next page.)

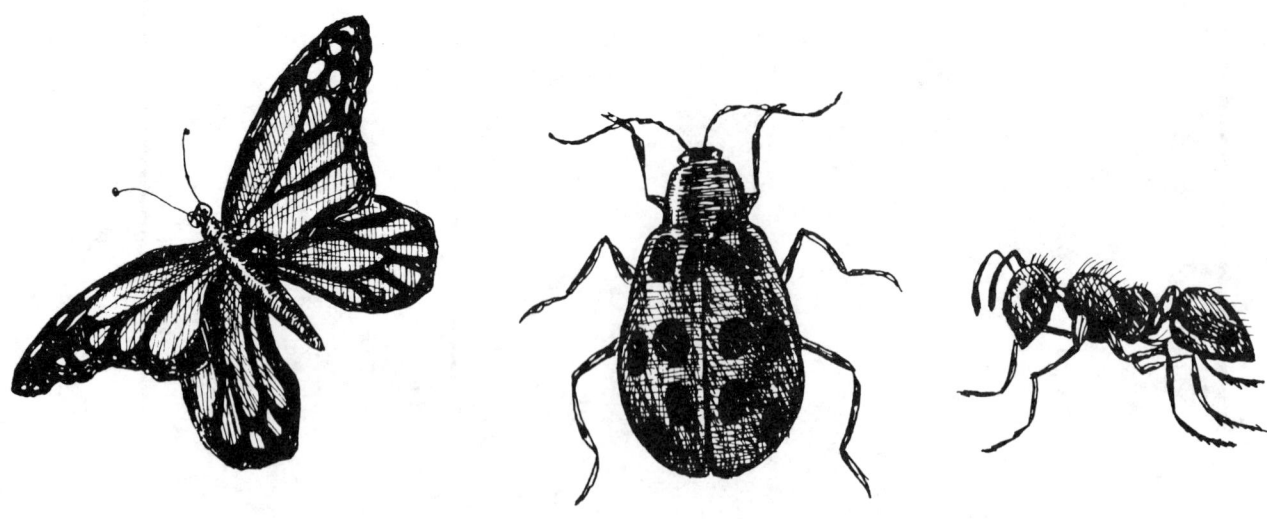

INSECT ROTATION LAB (cont'd.)

NO.	NAME	WINGS		NUMBER OF WINGS		CARRIES DISEASE		SOCIAL		DESTRUCTIVE	
		YES	NO	1 PR.	2 PR.	YES	NO	YES	NO	YES	NO
1.											
2.											
3.											
4.											
5.											
6.											
7.											
8.											
9.											
10.											
11.											
12.											
13.											
14.											
15.											
16.											
17.											
18.											
19.											
20.											
21.											
22.											
23.											
24.											
25.											

13

MOBILE CLASSIFICATION

PURPOSE: To use as an aid in the study of classifications.

MATERIALS: Cardboard, poster, or spray paint, dowels or coat hangers, and string

PROCEDURE: Construct a mobile showing the steps in the classification of a plant or animal. The first step on the mobile is the kingdom and the second is phylum; then class, order, family, genus, and species may be used if desired. Use tags for names, outlines of the animals, or a combination of both.

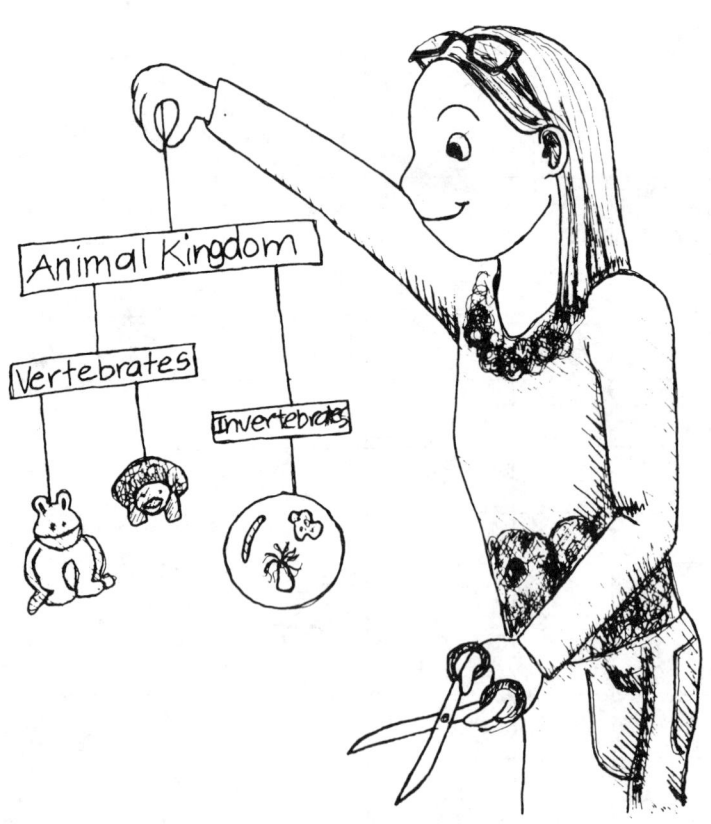

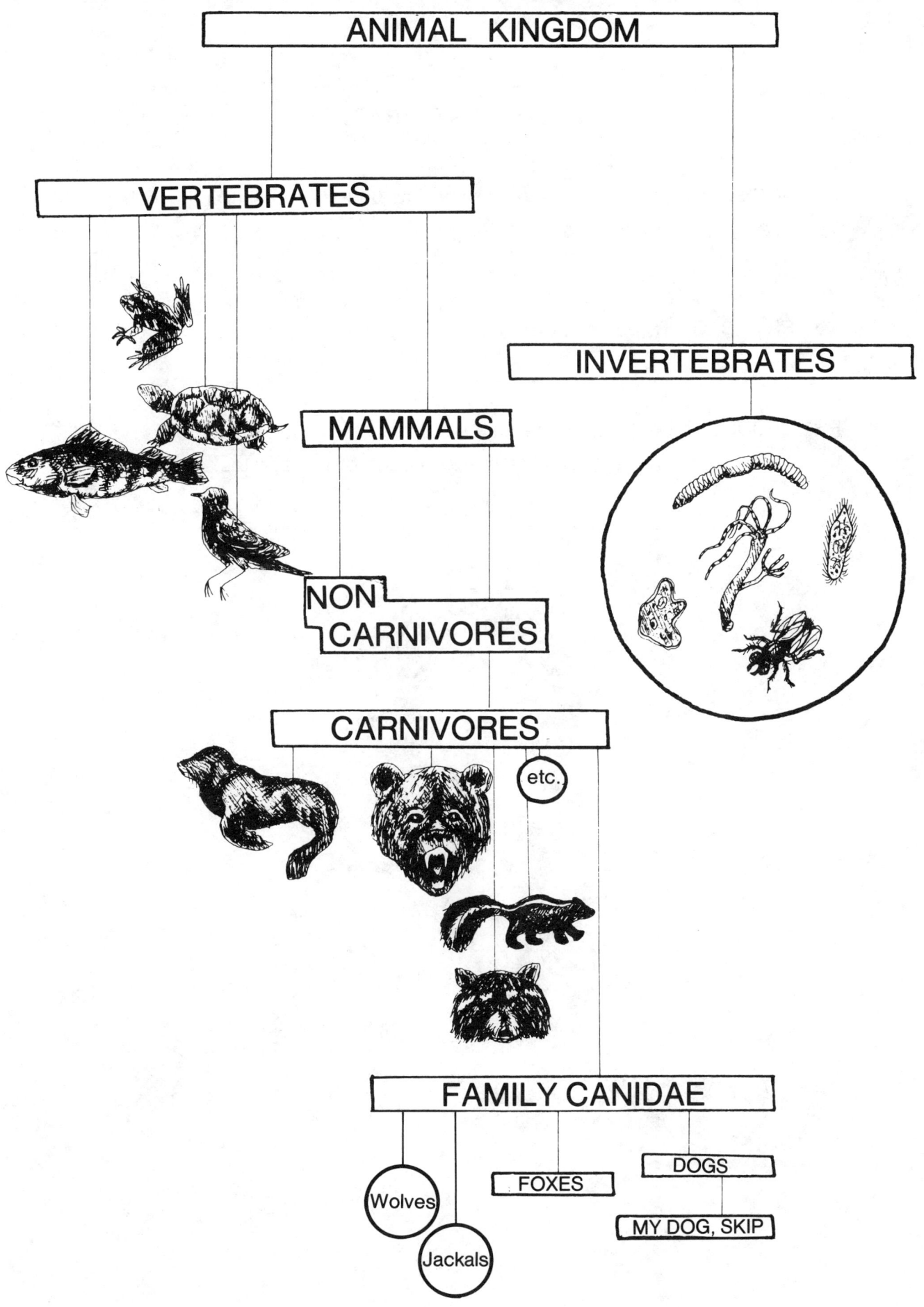

ANIMAL KINGDOM

VERTEBRATES

INVERTEBRATES

MAMMALS

NON CARNIVORES

CARNIVORES

etc.

FAMILY CANIDAE

Wolves

Jackals

FOXES

DOGS

MY DOG, SKIP

THE VERTEBRATES

PURPOSE: To contrast the differences and emphasize the similarities in the vertebrate groups of animals.

MATERIALS: Chart, pen or pencil

PROCEDURE: Fill in the spaces with the correct information which points out the similarities and differences in the five groups of vertebrates.

Young Fed Milk Yes or No					
Born Alive or Hatched					
Habitat— Tropics, Temperate, Arctic					
Important as Food Source for Man, Yes/No					
Number of Chambers in Heart					
Warm or Cold-Blooded					
Type of Appendages					
Type of Body Covering					
ANIMALS	FISH	AMPHIBIANS	REPTILES	BIRDS	MAMMALS

MAGIC TRIANGLE QUIZ

PURPOSE: To provide a frog quiz or review with an added mathematical interest.

MATERIALS: A magic triangle, lettered questions, and numbered answers

PROCEDURE: Have students place number answers to questions in each of the small lettered triangles. If answers are correct, each side of the large triangle will add up to 17. Use each number only once.

MAGIC TRIANGLE QUIZ

QUESTIONS:

a. To which class do frogs belong?

b. With what structures do tadpoles breathe?

c. What are the female reproductive organs of the frog?

d. What structure is present in mammals which a frog does not have?

e. How many chambers are in a frog's heart?

f. What are the male reproductive organs of a frog?

g. Which is the largest internal organ in a frog's body?

h. Which ducts lead from the kidneys to the bladder?

i. Through which ducts do eggs in a female frog pass?

ANSWERS:

1. amphibians
2. testes
3. oviducts
4. ureters
5. gills
6. ovaries
7. three

8. liver
9. diaphragm
10. reptiles
11. lungs
12. heart
13. gall bladder
14. four

QUESTIONS FOR DISCUSSION:

1. What are the two environments in which a frog lives?

2. How are the bodies of frogs adapted to these environments?

3. Describe the life cycle of a frog.

WHAT IS YOUR LIFE SCIENCE ESP?

PURPOSE: ESP refers to extrasensory perception. Those who believe in ESP are called sheep, while those who do not are called goats. Sheep consider ESP as a special gift which takes the form of knowledge of events before the events actually happen, perceiving objects not visible to the senses, or communication from one mind to another. Here is a little game which tests your "Life Science ESP."

MATERIALS: Two decks of 3" x 5" cards, each deck consisting of the following cards:

Mollusk Suit: 3" x 5" cards with an outline of a blue clam, a red clam, a blue snail, and a red snail. (One outline on each card, four cards to a suit.)

Arthropod Suit: 3" x 5" cards with outlines of a red butterfly, a blue butterfly, a red beetle, and a blue beetle.

Coelenterate Suit: 3" x 5" cards with outlines of a red hydra, a blue hydra, a red sea anemone, and a blue sea anemone.

Echinoderm Suit: 3" x 5" cards with outlines of a red starfish, a blue starfish, a red sand dollar, and a blue sand dollar.

Flatworm Suit: 3" x 5" cards with outlines of a blue planaria, a red planaria, a red tapeworm, and a blue tapeworm.

PROCEDURE: First of all, remember this is just a game. We are more interested in the probability of picking the correct cards than in whether the students are "sheep" or "goats." The subject to be tested spreads the four suits of cards in front of him, keeping the suits together but making sure all the outline drawings are visible. The person testing the subject's ESP selects a card at random from his shuffled deck. Holding the card in front of him or just thinking of the group—Mollusk, Arthropod, Coelenterate, Echinoderm, or Flatworm—the subject tries to guess, first, on which of the five groups the tester is concentrating. On chance alone, he has a one-in-five opportunity of picking the correct suit. Secondly, the subject guesses which of the two animals of the suit on which the tester is concentrating. On this guess the subject has a one-in-two chance of guessing correctly. Thirdly, the subject guesses the color of the card. This is also a one-in-two chance. The subject receives ten points for correctly guessing the animal, and two points for correctly guessing the color.

>
> 14 points—Excellent
>
> 12 points—Good
>
> 4 points—Fair to Poor
>
> 2 points—Very Poor
>
> 0 points—No ESP Shown This Game

The game only takes a few minutes to play and it should be repeated several times for each subject to determine whether scoring is consistent. A sample scorecard is provided on the next page.

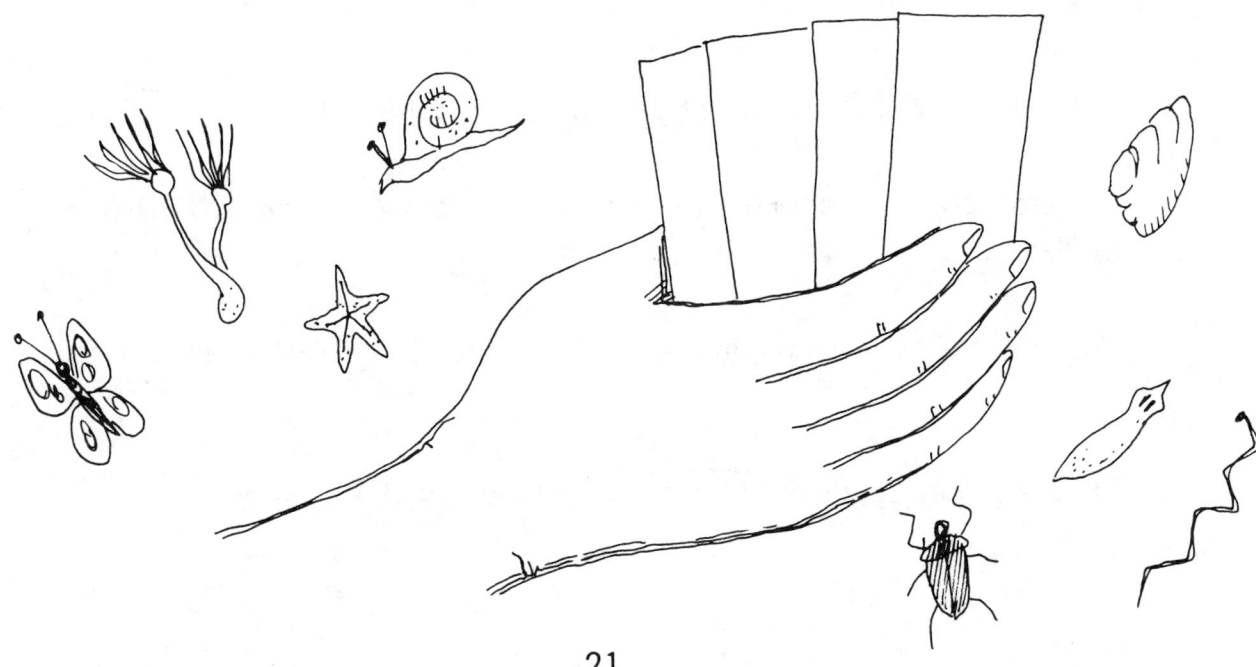

21

SAMPLE SCORECARD

Subject's Name _____

Tester's Name _____

Suit Correct . . . . 10 pts.
Name Correct . . . . 2 pts.
Color Correct . . . . 2 pts.

	Trial 1	Trial 2	Trial 3	Trial 4	Trial 5
Number of Points					

The probability of guessing the group (suit) to which the card belongs is 1 in 5 or 20%.

The probability of guessing the name of the animal (clam, snail) after guessing the suit is 1 in 2 or 50%.

The probability of guessing the color (red, blue) of the animal is 1 in 2 or 50%.

The probability of guessing all three questions is 1 in 20 or 5%.

The probability of guessing the suit and the name of the animal is 1 in 10 or 10%.

The probability of guessing the suit and the color of the animal is also 1 in 10 or 10%.

The probability of guessing the name and the color is 1 in 4 or 25%.

This card should be blue.

This card should be blue.

Coelenterate Suit (Hollow-Bodied Animals)

This card should be red.

This card should be red.

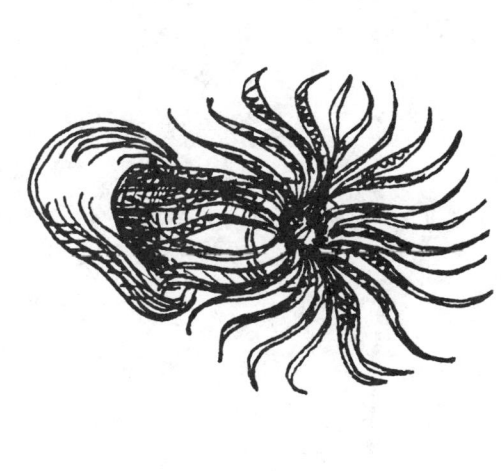

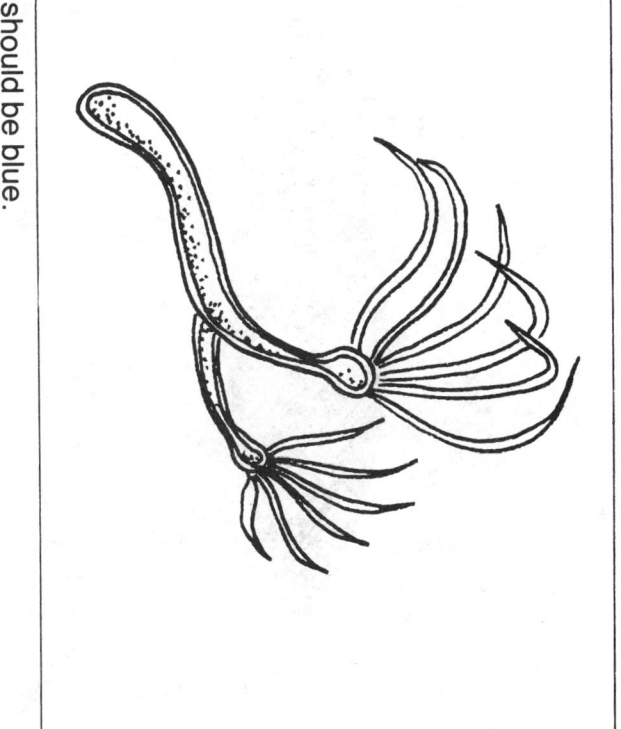

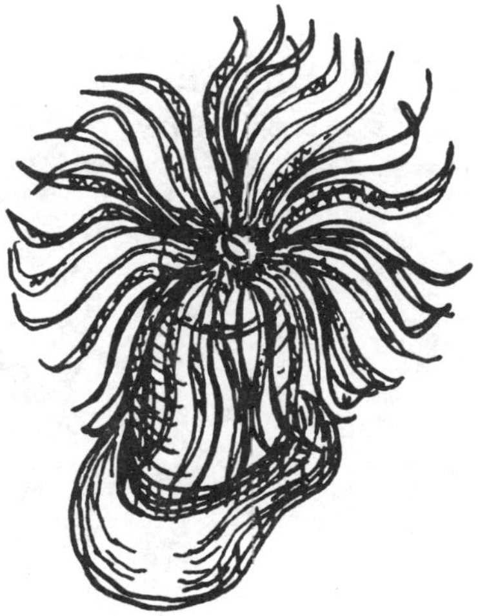

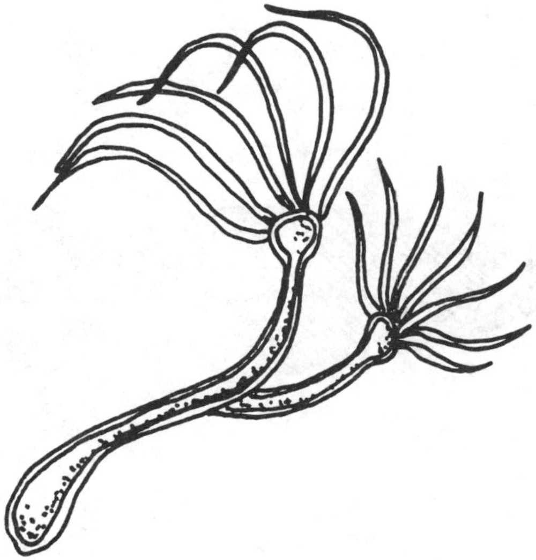

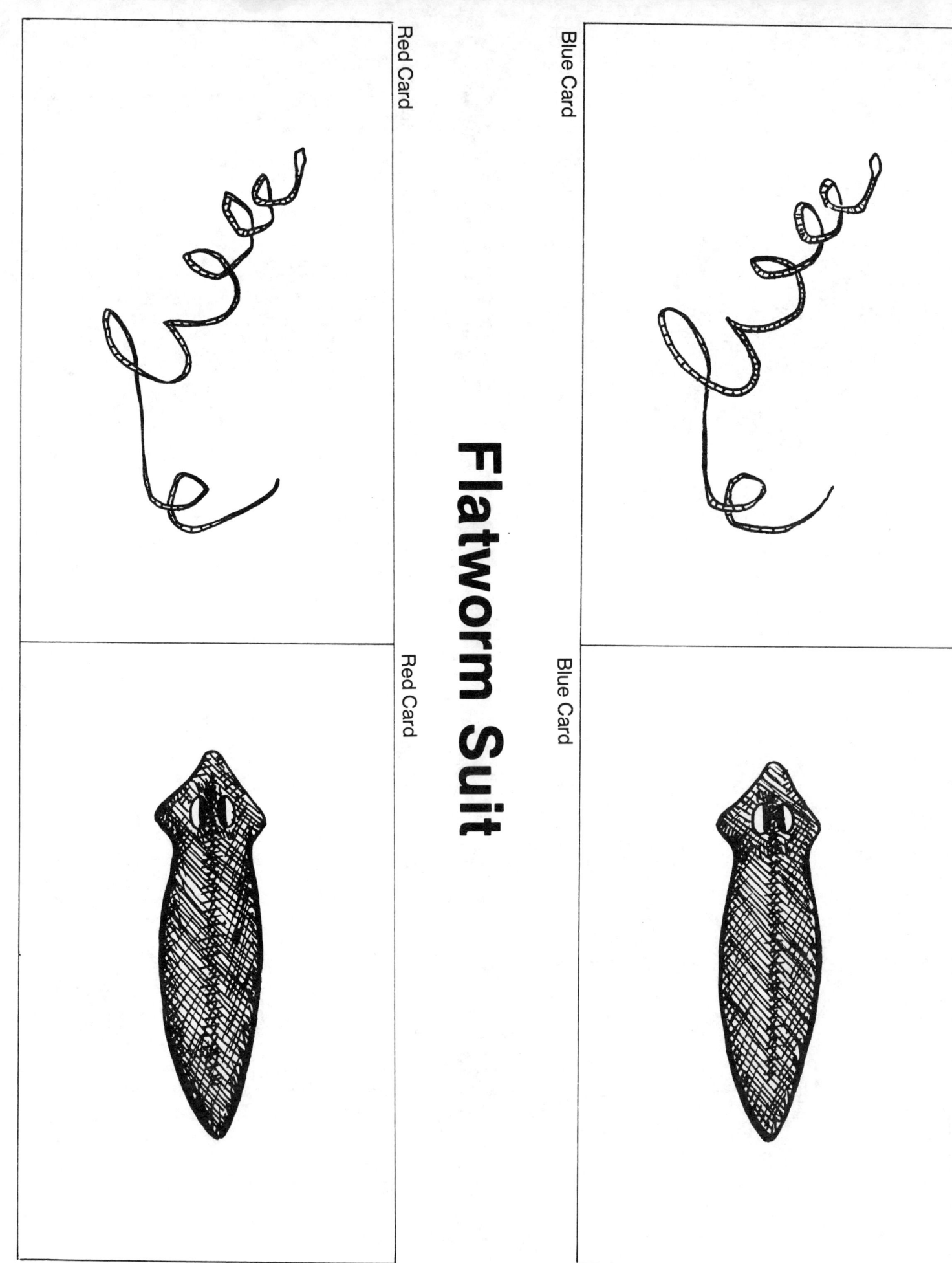

Flatworm Suit

Mollusk Suit (Soft-Bodied Animals)

25

Arthropod Suit (Jointed-Foot Animals)

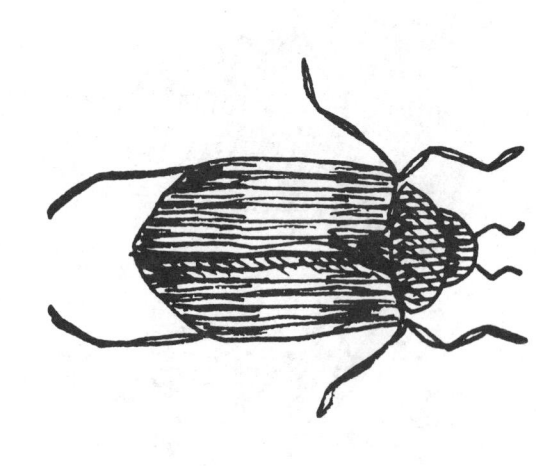

26

Blue Card

Blue Card

Echinoderm Suit (Spiny-Skinned Animals)

Red Card

Red Card

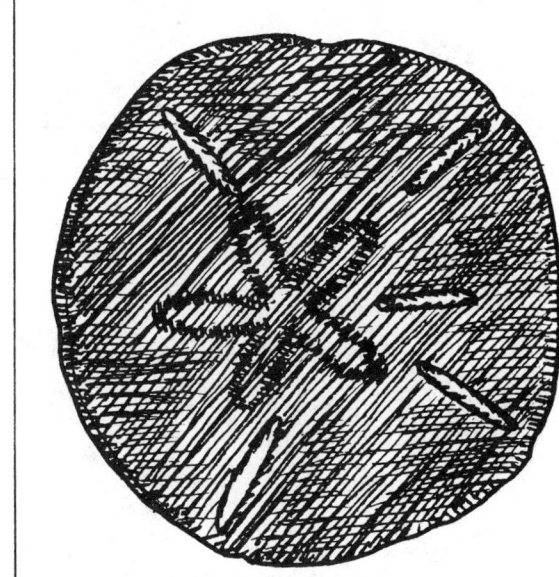

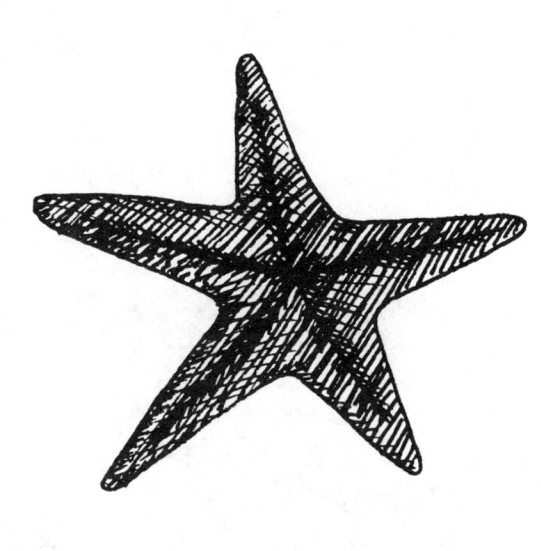

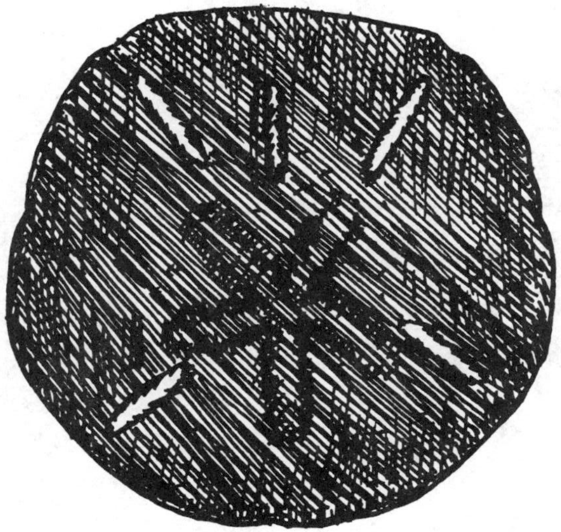

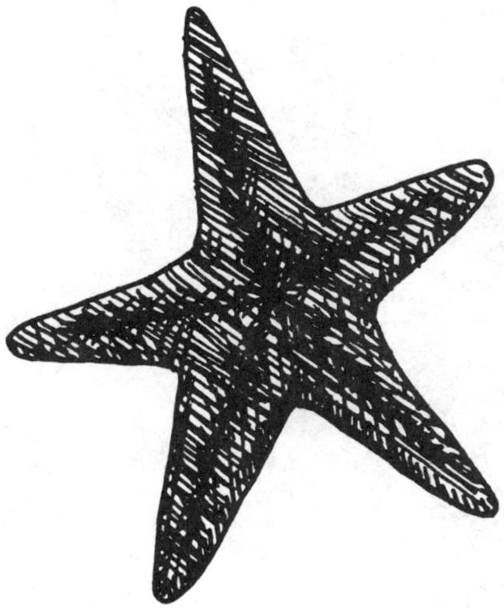

REPTILE KEY

PURPOSE: To give students practice in using a key; to familiarize students with the characteristics of reptiles.

MATERIALS: Pictures or drawings as provided on page 30

PROCEDURE: A key is a valuable tool to anyone interested in the identification of living things. In using a key a student takes all the information he is given about an object and follows the given steps. In order to find the name of the reptiles, always start at 1A for each reptile, determine if the description 1A or 1B fits, then follow down the key as directed by the guide words at the end of the line.

A SIMPLE REPTILE KEY

1A	Has a vertebral column fused into a shell	See 2
1B	Has no shell	See 3
2A	Shell apparent, feet with toes and claws	Tortoise
2B	Shell apparent, appendages formed into flippers	Leatherback Turtle
3A	Body legless	See 4
3B	Body with four appendages	See 5
4A	Head lance shaped, pit between the nostril and the eye	See 6
4B	Head not lance shaped, no pit between the nostril and the eye	See 7
5A	Body flat and beaded	Gila Monster
5B	Body not flat and beaded	See 8
6A	Hourglass design on back	Copperhead
6B	Diamond design on back	Diamondback Rattlesnake
7A	Body solid black in color	Racer Snake
7B	Body striped or designed	King Snake
8A	Body covered with large scaly skin, eyes and nostrils on top of the head	See 10
8B	Body covered with scales, eyes located at the sides of the head	See 9
9A	Ridge on dorsal side of the body	Iguana
9B	Ridge lacking	Chuckawalla
10A	Snout rounded	Alligator
10B	Snout pointed	Crocodile

CAN YOU CLASSIFY THESE REPTILES?

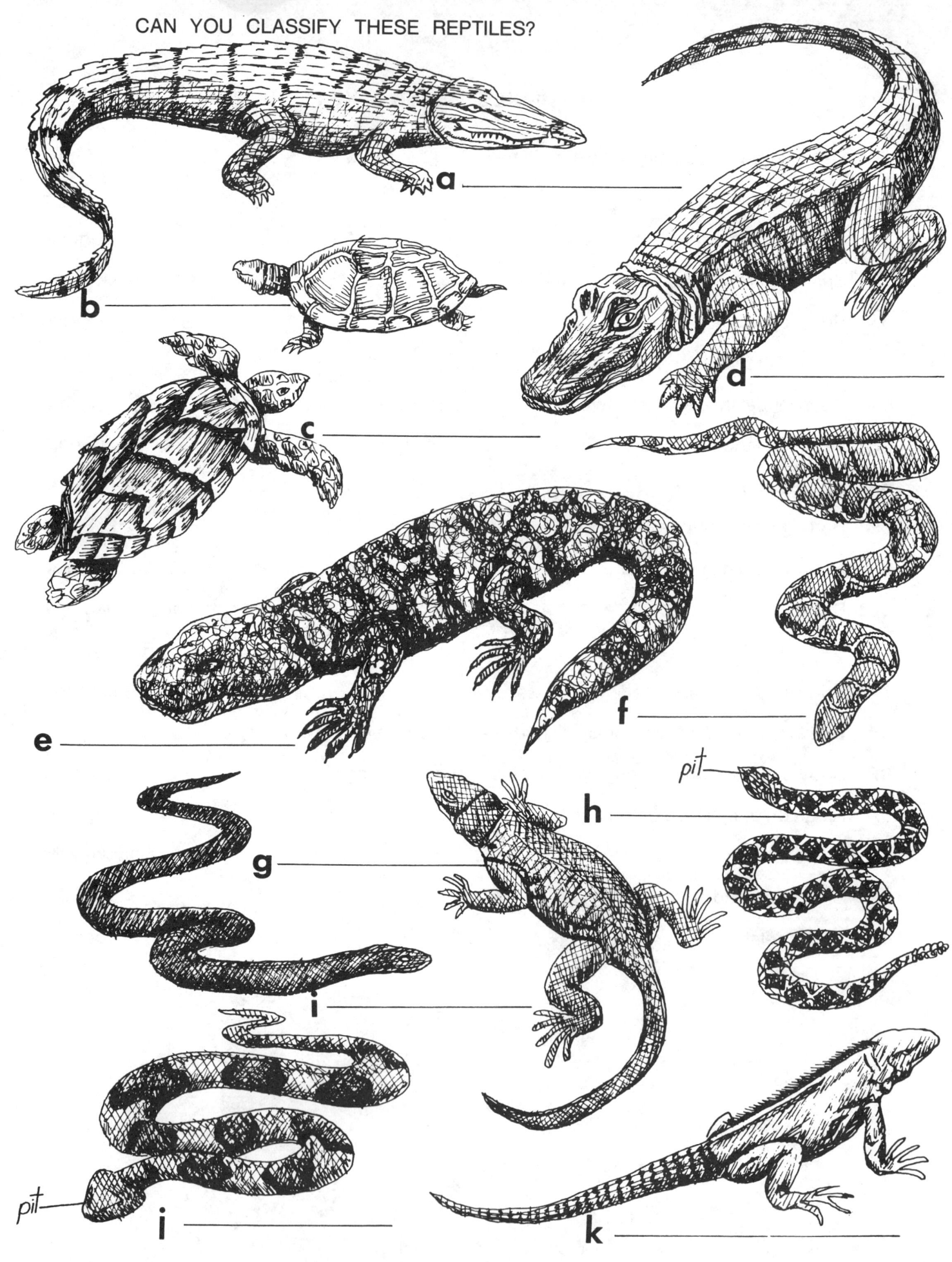

a _____

b _____

c _____

d _____

e _____

f _____

g _____

h _____

pit

i _____

pit

i _____

k _____

30

A PIT VIPER

PURPOSE: In the study of reptiles a knowledge of the most common types of poisonous snakes is not only of great interest, but it is also of great value. The following activity is designed to give students that information.

MATERIALS: A student drawing, a chart or a ditto sheet with the provided drawing of a pit viper's head

PROCEDURE: Discover the parts of a pit viper's head by matching the statements to the circles on the drawing (next page).

EXPLANATION: In the United States there are four types of poisonous snakes. They are the coral, the rattlesnake, the copperhead, and the cotton-mouth moccasin. Although poisonous, the coral snake is not a pit viper. Its range is limited to the deep south, and its poison (venom) is different from that of the pit vipers in that it attacks the nervous system (neurotoxin). In this activity we are primarily concerned with the head features of pit vipers. The pit vipers are the rattlesnakes, cottonmouth moccasins, and copperheads. The venom of a pit viper is a hemotoxin which breaks down the red corpuscles of the blood. The best known first aid for snake bite is suction. A suction cup should be used if available. The mouth can be used if no suction cup is available. Get medical attention for the victim at once.

HEAD OF A PIT VIPER

Put the number of the correct descriptive statement in the circle.

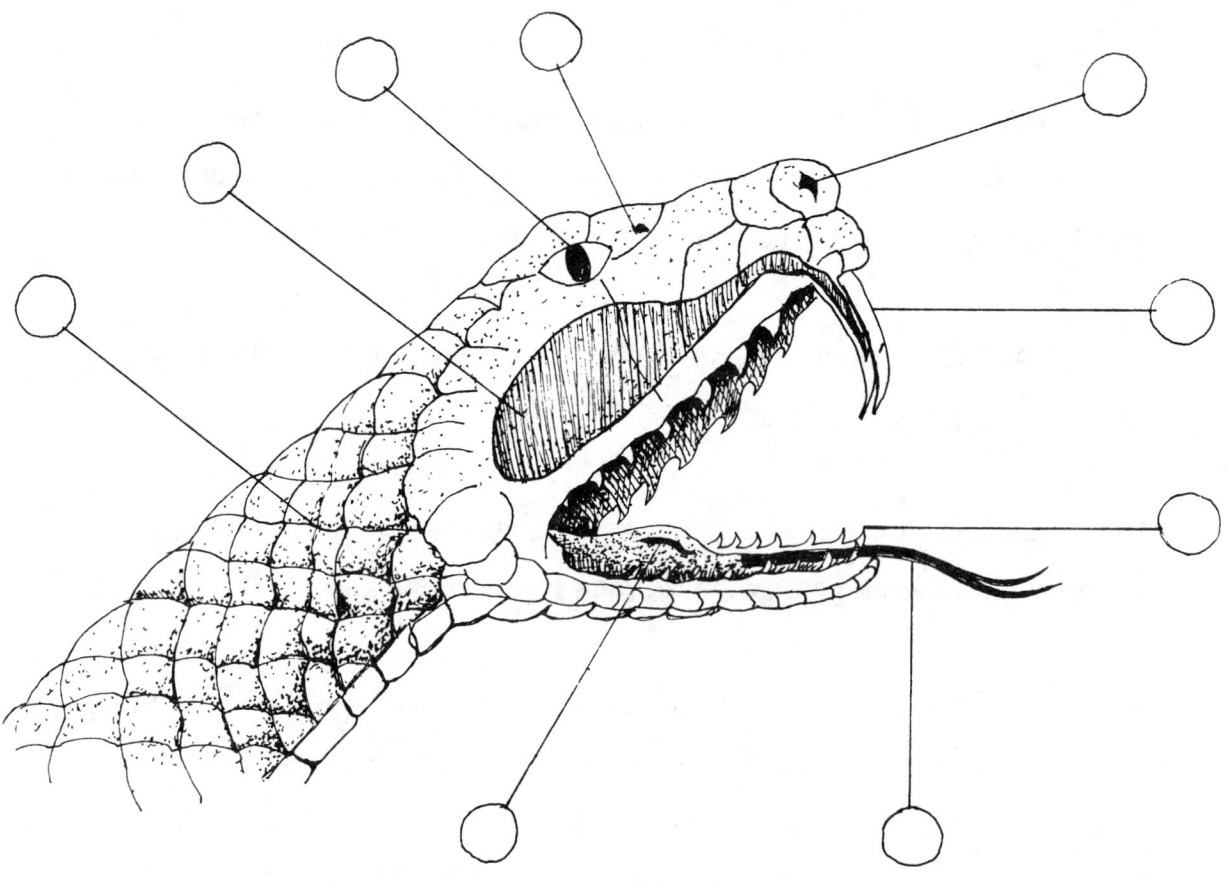

1. _____ Elliptical pupil of a pit viper's eye

2. _____ Scaly skin of a reptile

3. _____ Nostril

4. _____ A fang or hollow tooth

5. _____ Forked tongue, used to "taste" the air

6. _____ The glottis or opening to the trachea (windpipe)

7. _____ Solid teeth

8. _____ Venom sac

9. _____ The pit, a highly sensitive area

BIRD FLYWAYS

PURPOSE: While studying birds, it is beautiful to acquaint students with the major migratory bird routes of the United States and Canada.

MATERIALS: Maps of the United States and Canada, information on the four major flyways of the United States and Canada

PROCEDURE: The four migratory routes across North America are the Pacific Flyway, Central Flyway, the Mississippi Flyway, and the Atlantic Flyway. The Pacific Flyway extends from the northern and southern coasts of Alaska along the Pacific coast west of the Rockies and along the west coast of Mexico and Central America. The Central Flyway observes the formation of the Rocky Mountains, extending from Alaska to the east coast of Mexico. The Mississippi Flyway is along the river routes of Canada, across the Great Lakes, and continuing south along the Mississippi and Missouri Rivers to the Louisiana coast. The Atlantic Flyway extends along the eastern coast of Canada and the United States, continuing along the eastern coast of Florida and into the West Indies. On a map of the United States and Canada, have the students make a key to represent the four flyways. Then, using their own key, mark the flyways on the outline maps provided for this purpose.

FLYWAYS OF NORTH AMERICA

BIRDS OF THE UNITED STATES

PURPOSE: To learn more about birds through the observation and study of their habits. This can be done at home, on a field trip, or in class by the use of bird books, bird cards, etc.

MATERIALS: Bird books, bird cards, magazine articles about birds, etc., pen or pencil, data sheet

PROCEDURE: Observe and identify birds, estimate size, record other information observed.

BIRDS OF THE UNITED STATES (cont'd.)

NAME	SIZE	BREEDING PLACE	FOODS	AREAS INHABITED
1.				
2.				
3.				
4.				
5.				
6.				
7.				
8.				
9.				
10.				
11.				
12.				
13.				
14.				
15.				
16.				
17.				
18.				
19.				
20.				
21.				
22.				
23.				
24.				
25.				
26.				
27.				
28.				
29.				
30.				

WHAT IS YOUR OUTDOOR I.Q.?

PURPOSE: To stimulate interest in our rich heritage of the outdoors, its wildlife, and the various habitats.

MATERIALS: Animal drawings and their corresponding tracks. The drawings or pictures may be put on cards to be matched up with cards of the animal's tracks.

PROCEDURE: With each animal give a hint as to its habitat or use of its limbs which would enable the student to match the animal to its tracks.

WHAT IS YOUR OUTDOOR I.Q.?

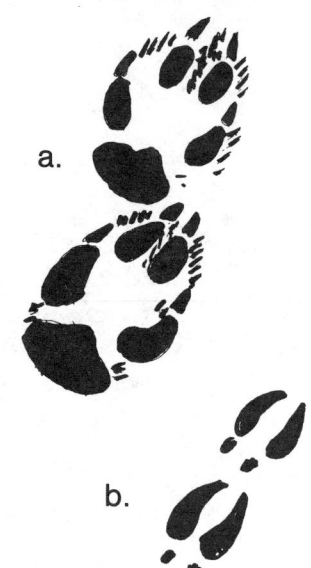

This animal is a bobcat. It has retractable claws. See if you can pick out its tracks.

a.

1._____

This animal is a grey squirrel. Its little feet are adapted for climbing trees. Find its tracks.

b.

2._____

This is a wolf. Its tracks are very similar to its relative, the dog. You have often seen a dog's tracks. See if you can find the tracks.

c.

3._____

This is a beaver. It spends much of its time in the water. Which tracks show an advantage to being in the water?

d.

4._____

This is a deer. It has hooves instead of toes. Which tracks belong to the deer?

e.

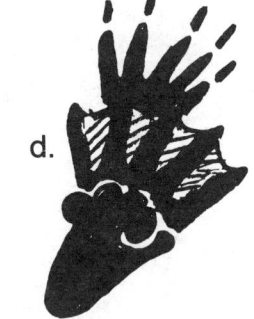

5._____

WHAT IS YOUR OUTDOOR I.Q.?

a.

This large mammal is a bear. It has four feet with claws on each paw. Can you find its tracks?

1._____

This is a skunk. Its hind feet leave a print which resembles a human's. Which tracks belong to the skunk?

2._____

b.

This is a caribou. It has tracks which are similar to a deer's. Which tracks belong to the caribou?

3._____

c.

This is a fox. Along with a wolf, it is related to a dog. Its tracks are similar to a dog's.

d.

4. _____

This is a rabbit. Its feet are like little snowshoes, well adapted for running in the snow. Which tracks belong to the rabbit?

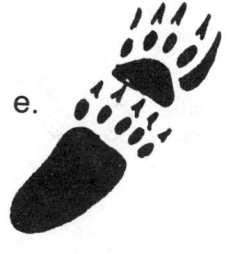

e.

5. _____

THE MOST COMMONLY STUDIED ANIMALS

PURPOSE: To provide guide sheets for the most commonly studied or dissected animals in biology and life science classes.

MATERIALS: Guide sheets, pen or pencil

PROCEDURE: These sheets can be used as they are or in conjunction with dissection activities. The activity sheets can be found on the following 12 pages.

Amoeba

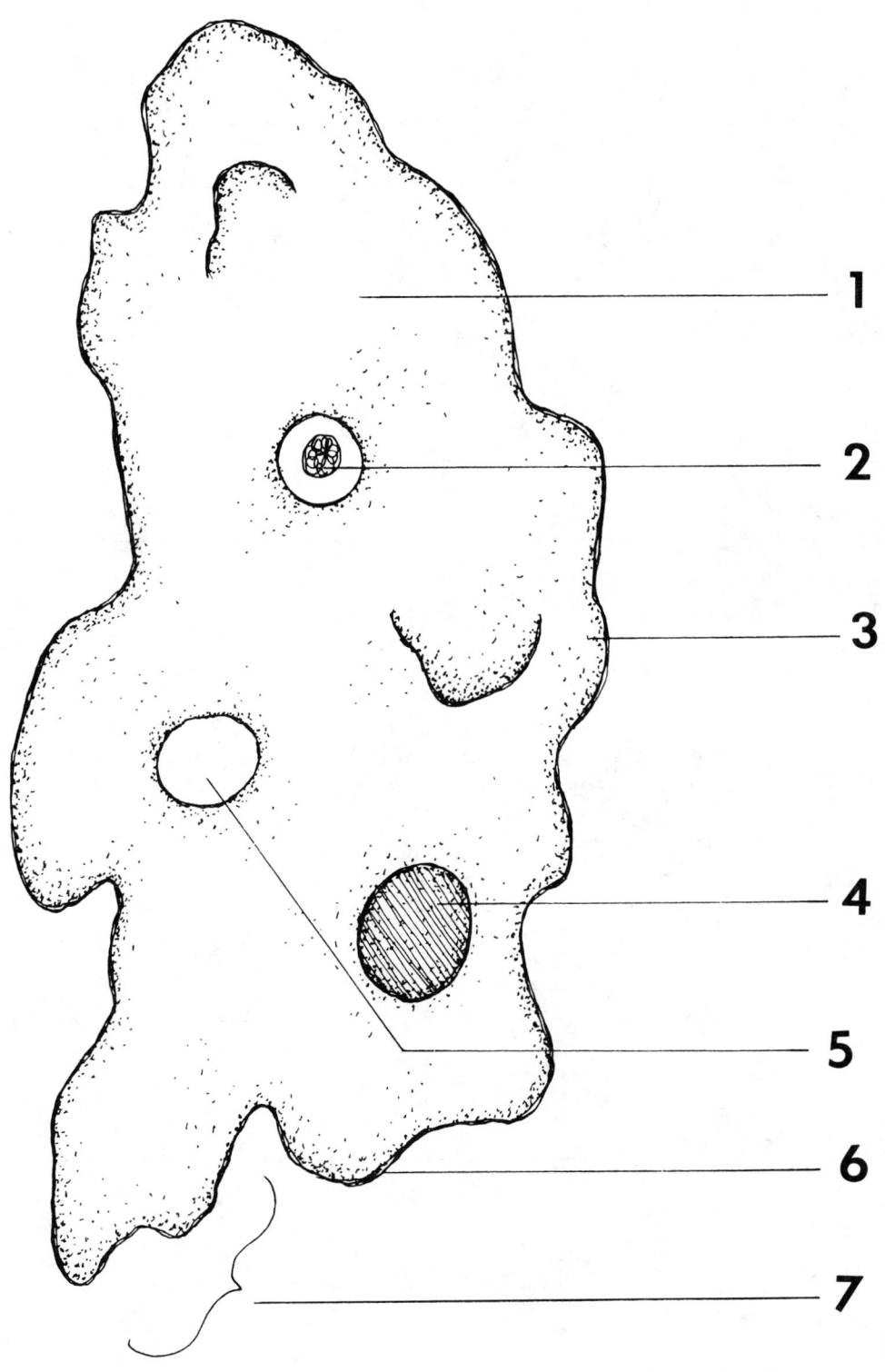

1

2

3

4

5

6

7

41

Euglena

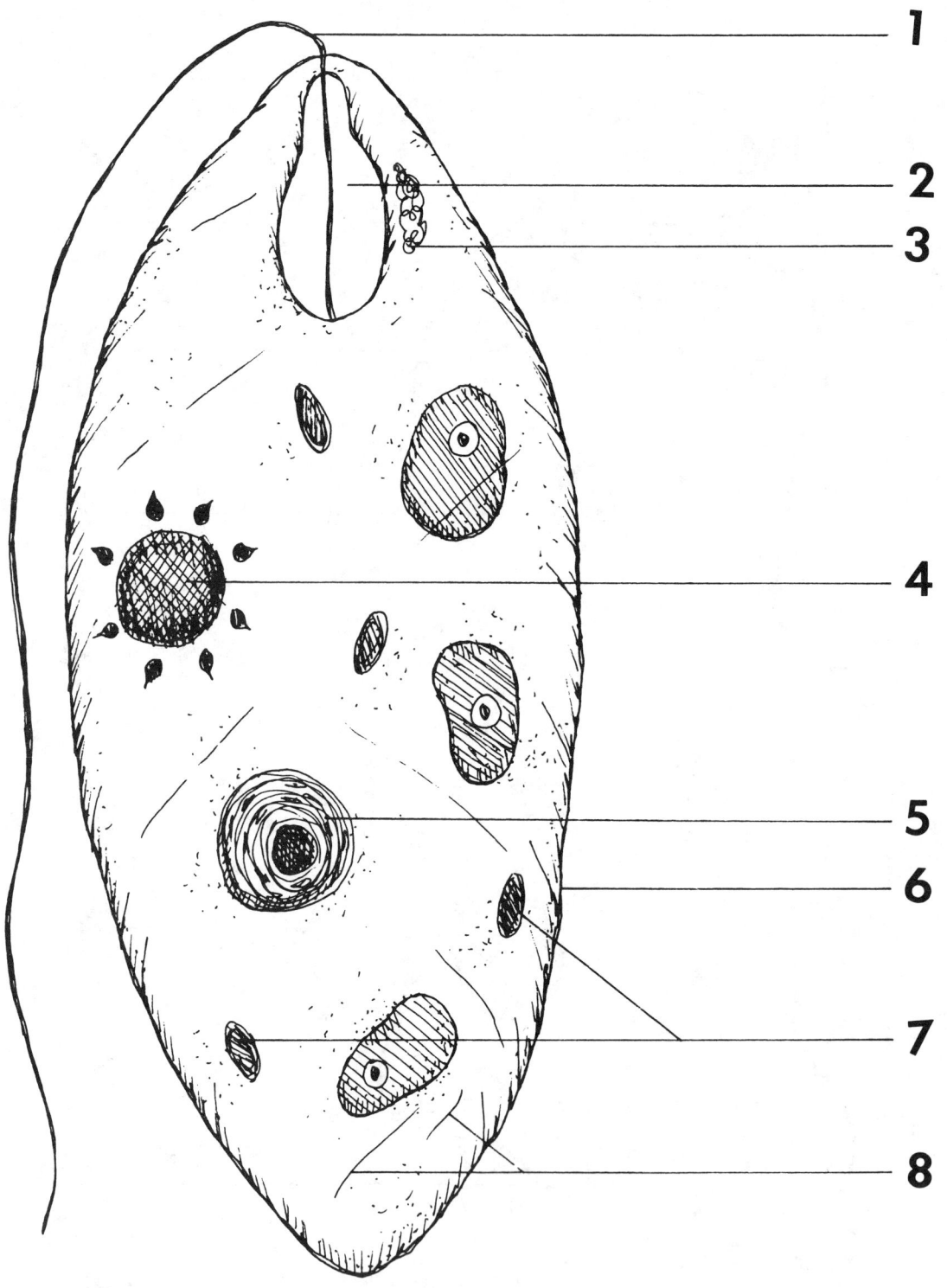

1

2

3

4

5

6

7

8

Paramecium

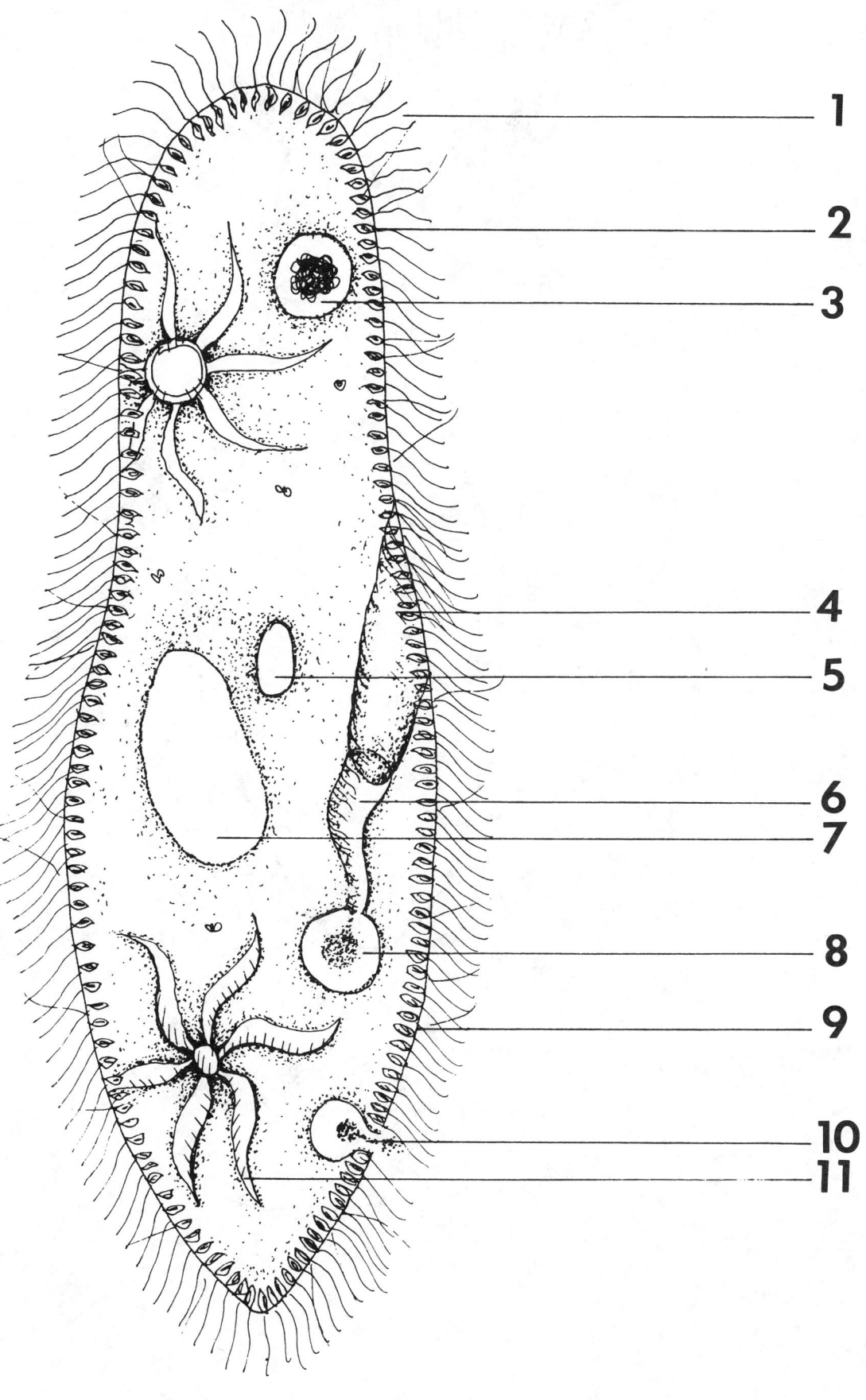

1

2

3

4

5

6

7

8

9

10

11

Sponge

1

2

3

4

5

Hydra

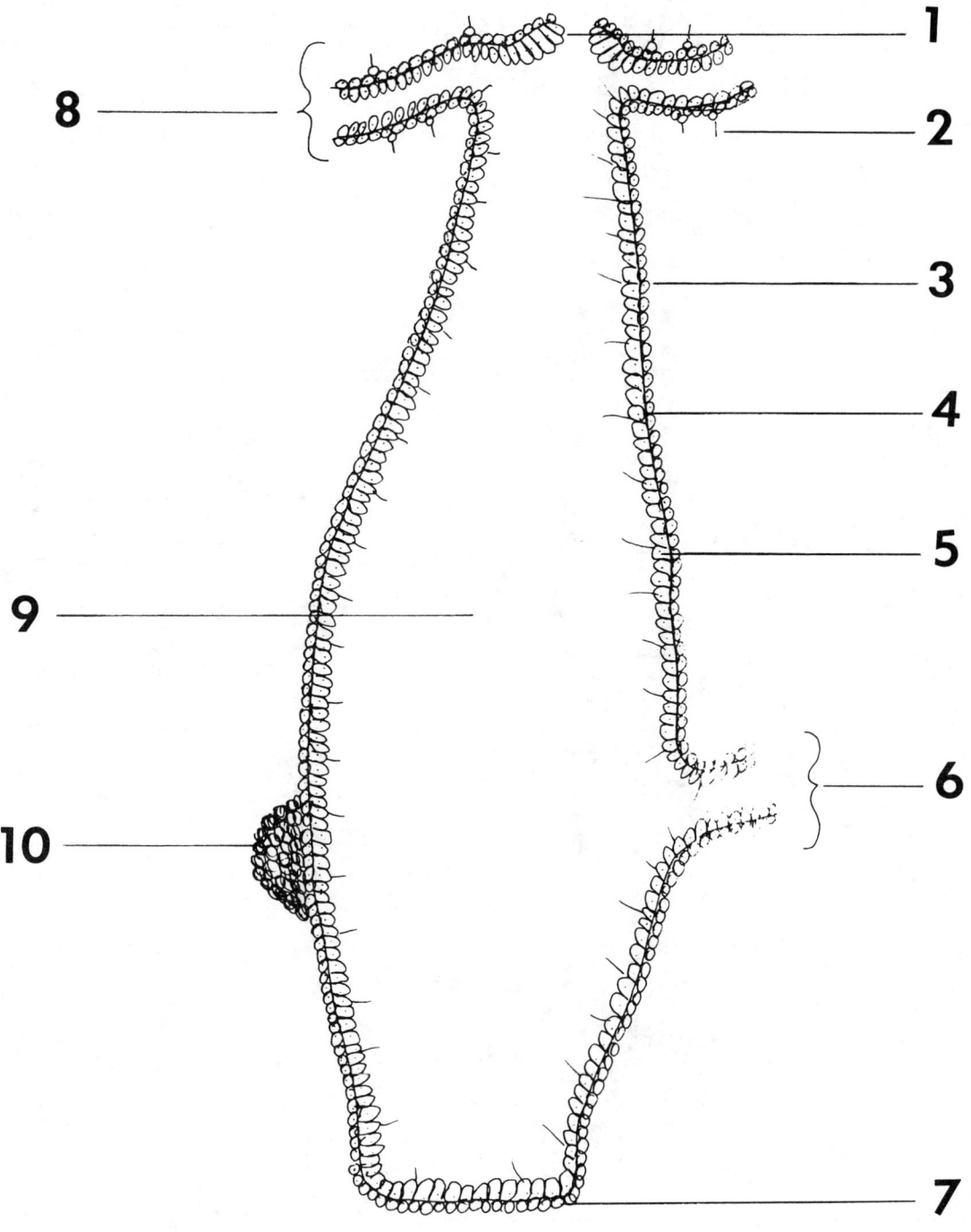

8

9

10

1

2

3

4

5

6

7

Planaria

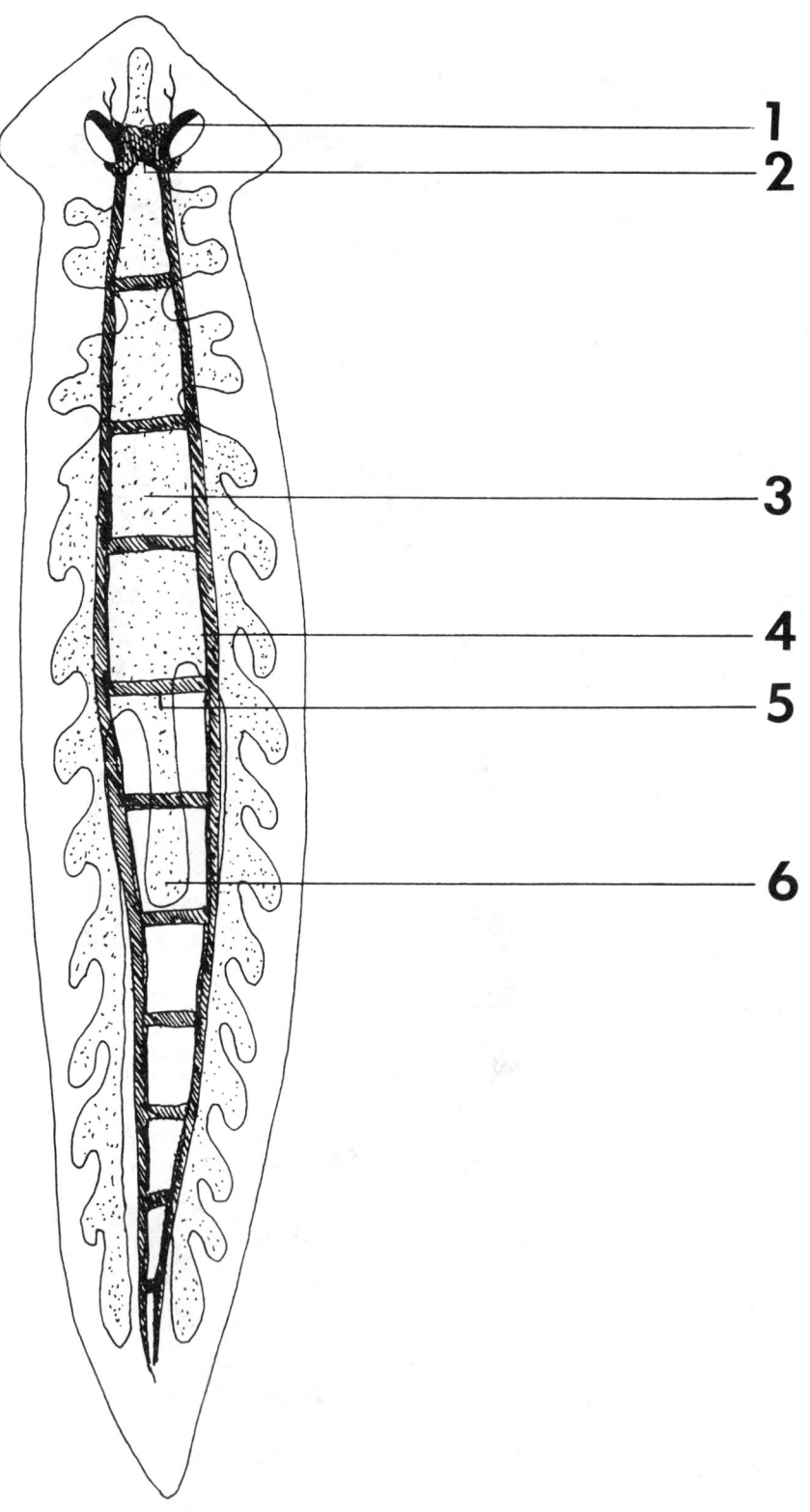

1

2

3

4

5

6

Earthworm—Digestive System

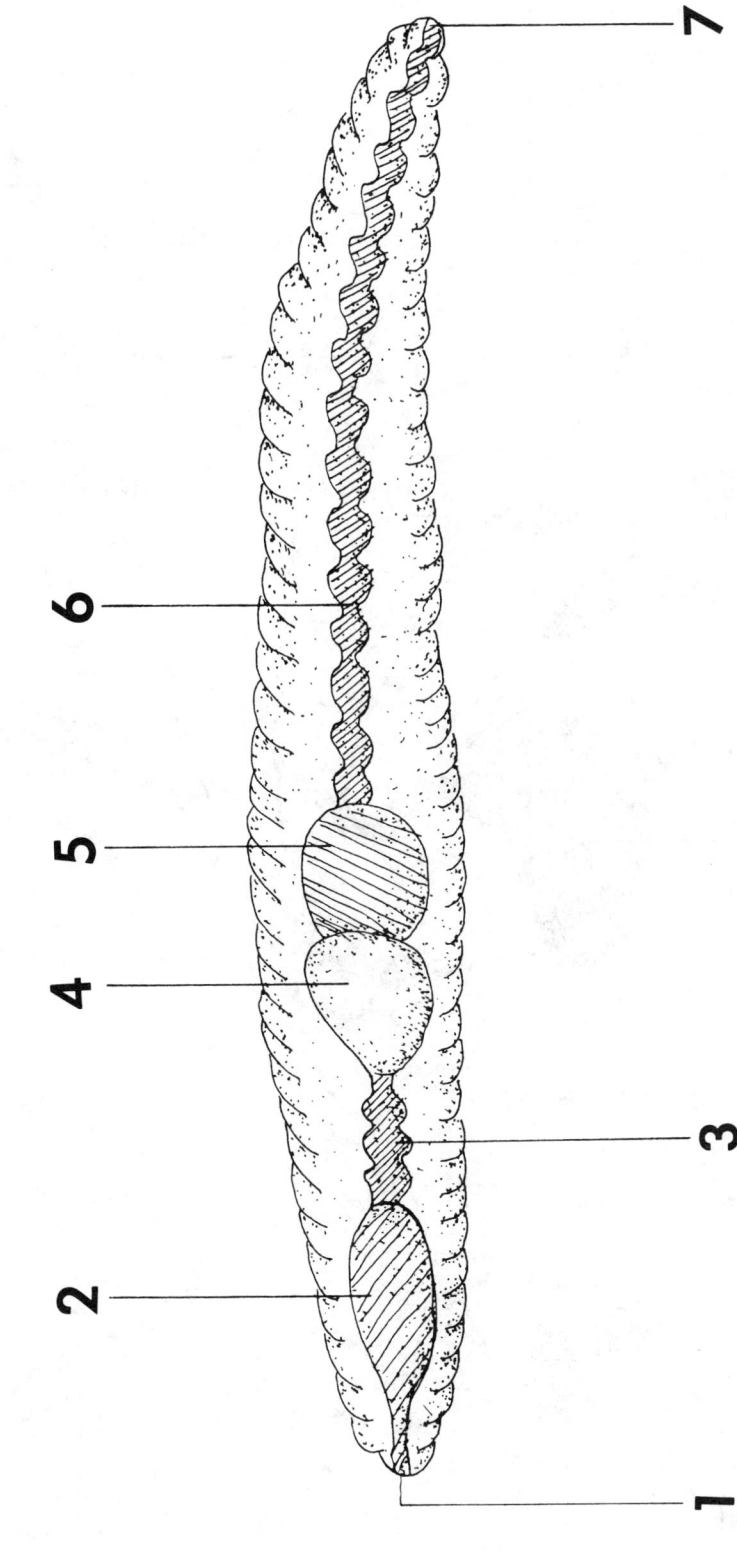

Grasshopper—External

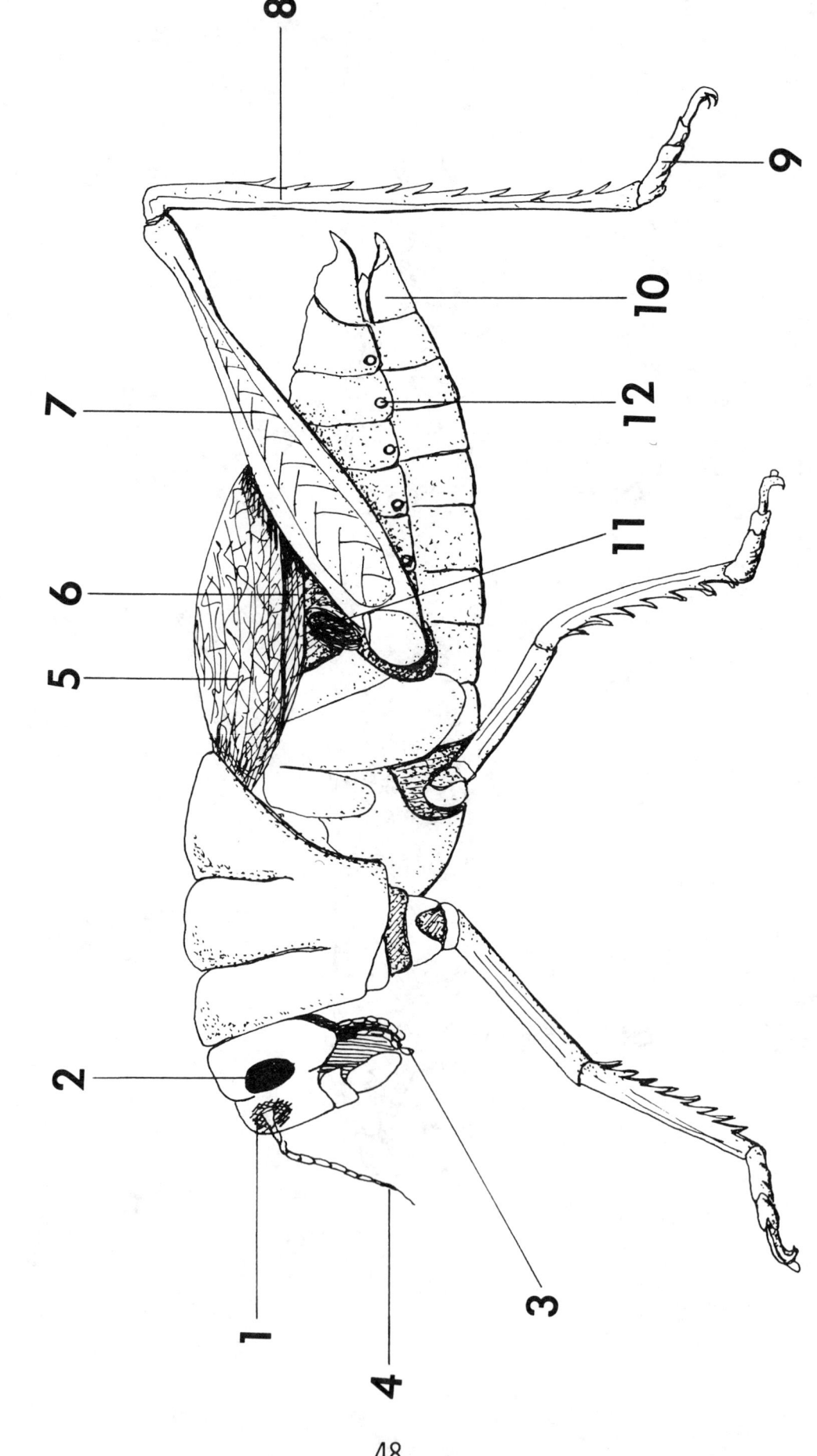

Grasshopper—Internal

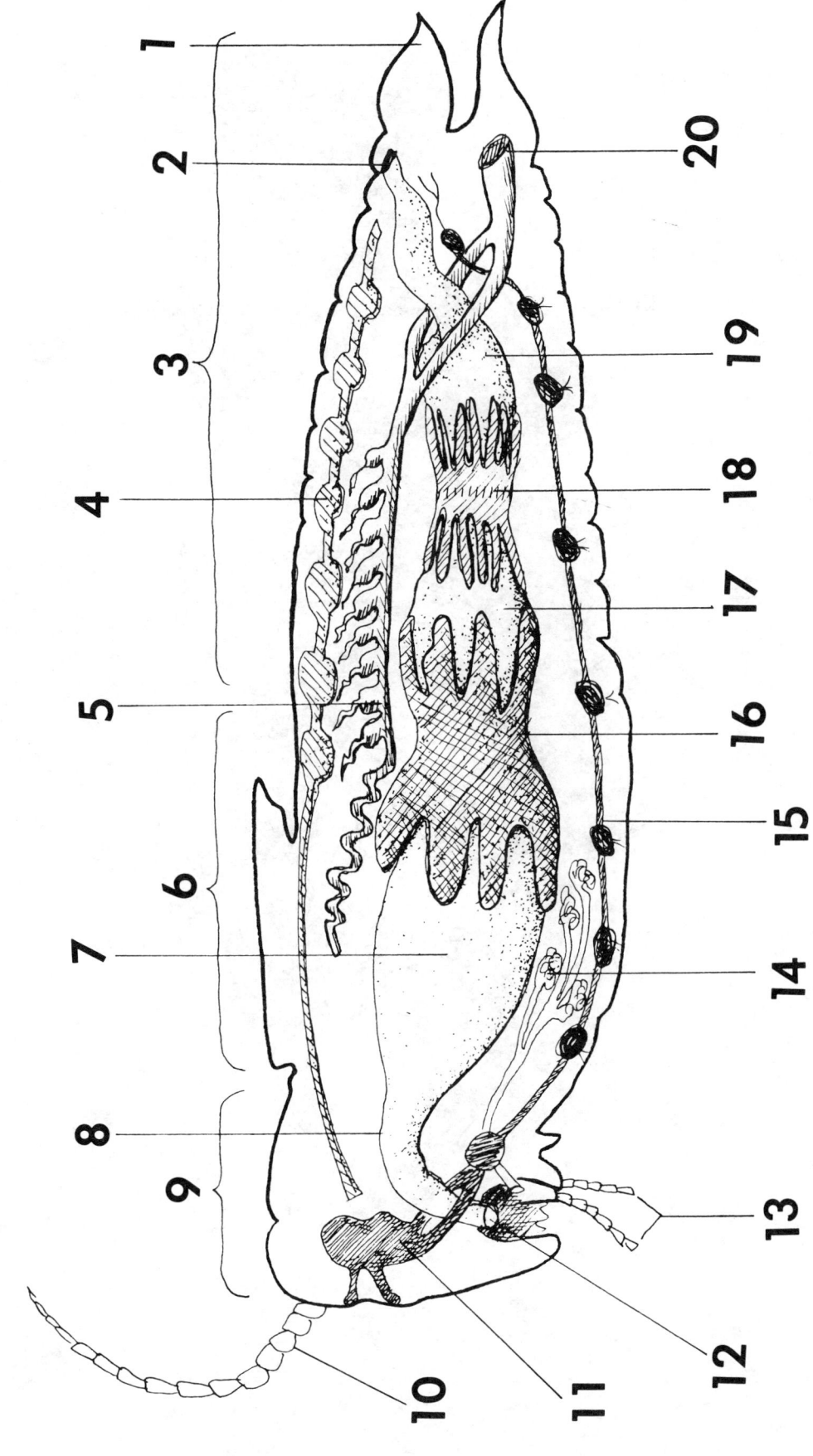

Fish—External

Fish—Internal

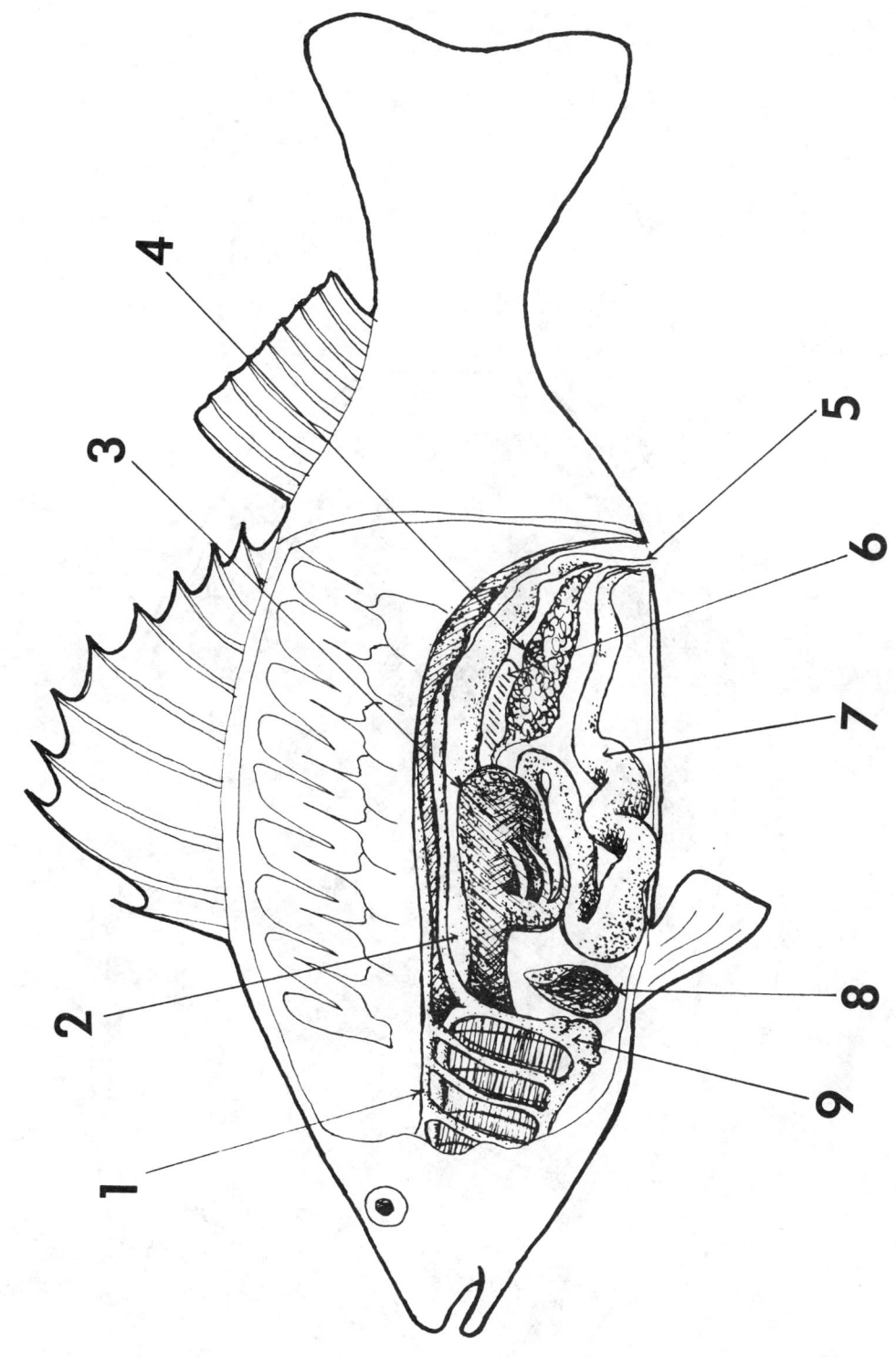

Frog—Internal

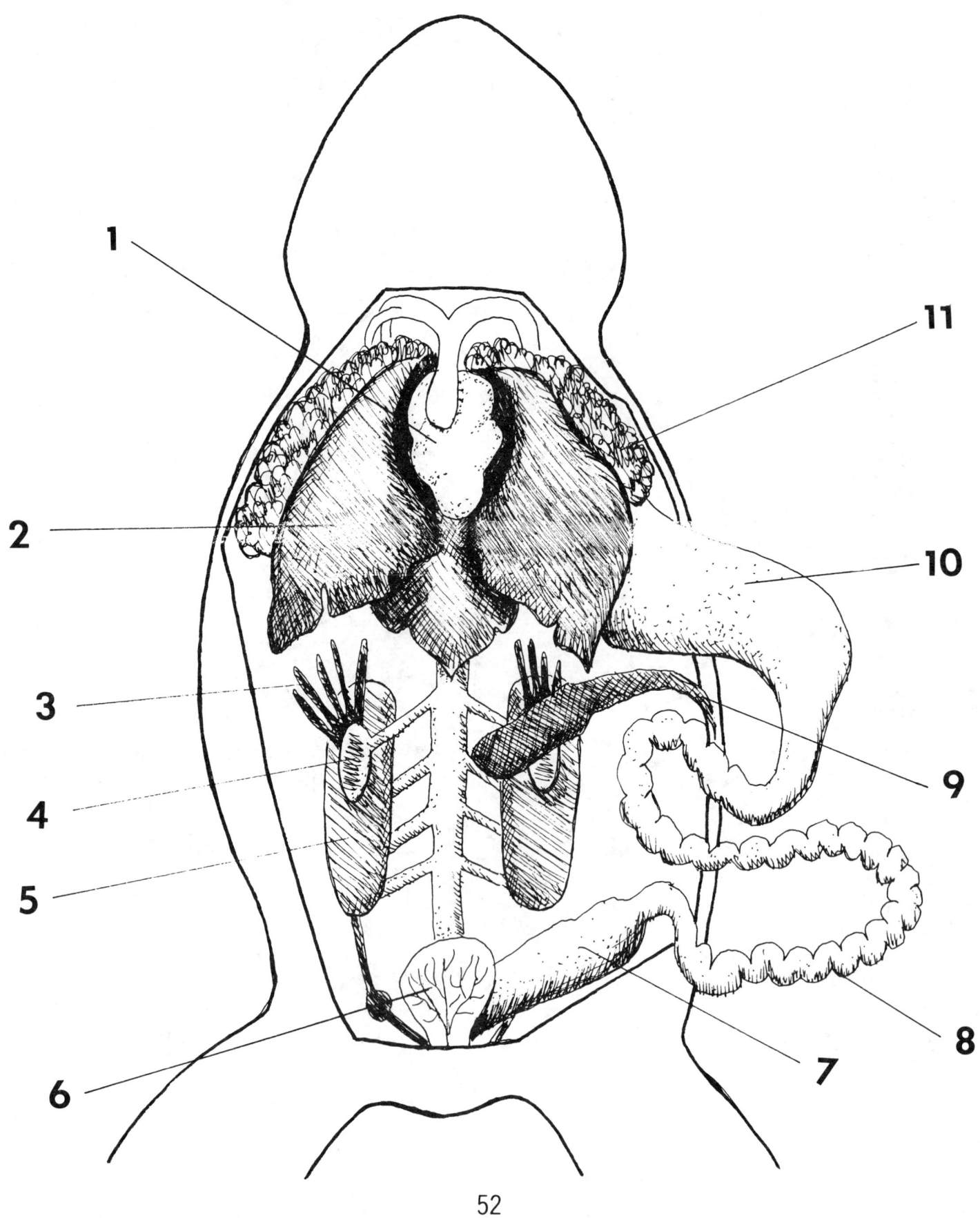

1

11

2

10

3

4

9

5

6

7

8

DO YOU KNOW SOME OF THE BRANCHES OF SCIENCE?

PURPOSE: To become acquainted with some of the specialized sciences dealing with living things.

MATERIALS: A list of some of the branches of biology and their definitions for matching

PROCEDURE: Match the book to the definition. This activity is continued on the next page.

QUESTIONS FOR DISCUSSION:

1. Many of the branches of science have the same word ending. What is it?

2. What is such an ending of a word called?

3. What do you think this ending means?

4. Do any of the branches of science begin with familiar words? If so, what are these words?

BRANCHES OF SCIENCE

1._____ Histology

2._____ Parasitology

3._____ Ichthyology

4._____ Bacteriology

5._____ Taxonomy

6._____ Physiology

7._____ Biology

8._____ Botany

9._____ Zoology

10._____ Entomology

11. _____ Microbiology

12. _____ Biochemistry

13. _____ Herpetology

14. _____ Paleontology

15. _____ Genetics

16. _____ Embryology

17. _____ Anatomy

18. _____ Ecology

19. _____ Anthropology

20. _____ Ornithology

* * * * *　* * * * *　* * * * *　* * * * *　* * * * *　* * * * *　* * * * *

a. The study of parasites

b. Study of plants

c. Science of classification of living things

d. Study of the transmission of traits from one generation to another

e. Study of birds

f. Study of the interrelationships of living things to their surroundings

g. Study of the structures of living things

h. Study of living things

i. The study of behavior of man

j. The study of the chemistry of living substances and processes

k. The study of reptiles and amphibians

l. The science which deals with microorganisms and their effects on other forms of life

m. The study of the microscopic structure of animal and plant tissue

n. The science which deals with the formation, early growth, and development of living organisms

o. Study of bacteria

p. Study of fish

q. Science which deals with ancient forms of life

r. The study of insects

s. The study of animals

t. The study of living functions and processes

PET SHOP

PURPOSE: This little game can be played when there are just a few minutes left at the end of a period or after a test.

MATERIALS: None

PROCEDURE: One person begins by saying, "My father has a pet shop and he sells _____." The word can begin with any animal whose name begins with an "A" such as alligator, albatross, etc. The second student says the same sentence but his animal's name must begin with a "B" and so on. Each student has a given time limit of 15 to 30 seconds and must pass if he cannot think of a pet in that amount of time. The game can be varied and become more complex by restricting the pets to birds, fish, etc.

MAMMAL BINGO

PURPOSE: To arouse interest in the study of mammals and to acquaint students with the names of a variety of mammals.

MATERIALS: A bingo sheet (next page), pencil or pen

PROCEDURE: The students are given sheets such as the sample on the next page. From the variety of names at the top of the sheet, they select their favorite mammals and write their names in the spaces. In this way each student will have a different sheet from his classmates. The teacher or a designated student will call the names of the mammals which have been copied on strips of paper and placed in a container. Crossing five spaces in a row or diagonally results in bingo. Students cross out names as they are called.

VARIATION: The students will enjoy playing "Blackout," which is filling all the spaces on the card. This can be done after playing a game of regular bingo. Just continue until the card is entirely covered.

MAMMAL BINGO (cont'd.)

Choose your favorite mammals and write their names in the spaces below.

armadillo	brown rat	bear	cacomistle
camel	caribou	cat	coati
cottontail	cougar	coyote	deer
dog	dolphin	elk	ermine
ferret	fox	horse	goat
hare	gopher	groundhog	jack rabbit
jaguar	killer whale	lemming	leopard
lion	lynx	man	marten
mink	mouse	mule	moose
muskrat	musk ox	ox	panther
pig	pika	polecat	porcupine
porpoise	puma	raccoon	rat
reindeer	sable	sea cow	sea lion
sheep	shrew	skunk	squirrel
tiger	walrus	weasel	whale
wolf	woodchuck	zebra	zebu

		FREE		

ANIMAL RECORDS

PURPOSE: To have students test their knowledge of various records held by animals.

MATERIALS: Questions such as those found on the following page. The questions should concern the records held by various animals.

PROCEDURE: The questions can be given on a ditto sheet or orally.

QUESTIONS:

1. Which is the largest and heaviest sea animal?
2. Which is the longest animal?
3. Which is the tallest animal?
4. Which animal has the longest life expectancy?
5. Which animal is the fastest?
6. What animal lays the largest egg?
7. Which animal has the heaviest brain?
8. What animal has the largest eye?
9. What is the largest land animal?
10. What is the smallest mammal?
11. What is the fastest mammal?
12. Which mammal has the longest life expectancy?
13. What animal has the longest gestation period?
14. What animal has the shortest gestation period?
15. What is the largest bird?
16. What is the smallest bird?
17. Which bird has the longest wing span?
18. Which bird is the fastest swimmer?
19. Which snake is the longest?
20. Which snake is the most poisonous?

You or your students can develop additional questions. The students might enjoy trying to discover a "record question" that would really challenge the other students.

ANSWER KEY

Page 6   Worm Key
- A. Ascaris
- B. Planaria
- C. Earthworm
- D. Tapeworm
- E. Leech
- F. Sandworm

Page 7   Live Earthworm Lab
- 1-6. Answers will vary.
- 7. Underneath—ventral side
- 8. Movement
- 9-13. Answers will vary.
- 14. Approximately 130 segments
- 15. Answers will vary.
- 16. a,c,d,f, and g should be circled.

Page 10   Symmetry
1. Whale, bilateral
2. Frog, bilateral
3. Snake, bilateral
4. Bat, bilateral
5. Sand Dollar, radial
6. Dragonfly, bilateral
7. Walrus, bilateral
8. Starfish, radial
9. Goose, bilateral
10. Fly, bilateral
11. Brittle Star, radial
12. Sea Urchin, radial

Page 17   The Vertebrates

Young Fed Milk — Yes or No	No	No	No	No	Yes
Born Alive or Hatched	Hatched, Some Born Alive	Hatched	Hatched, Some Born Alive	Hatched	Born Alive
Habitat — Tropics, Temperate, Arctic	All	Temperate, Tropics	Temperate, Tropics	All	All
Important as Food Source for Man— Yes or No	Yes	No	No	Yes	Yes
Number of Chambers in Heart	2	3	3 4 (A Few)	4	4
Warm or Cold-Blooded	Cold	Cold	Cold	Warm	Warm
Type of Appendages	Fins	Limbs	Some Have Limbs	Wings, Limbs	Limbs
Type of Body Covering	Scales	Skin	Scaly Skin	Feathers	Hair or Fur
ANIMAL	FISH	AMPHIBIAN	REPTILE	BIRD	MAMMAL

Page 18   Magic Triangle Quiz
1a, 5b, 6c, 9d, 7e, 2f, 8g, 4h, 3i

Page 30   A Simple Reptile Key
- a. Crocodile
- b. Tortoise
- c. Leatherback Turtle
- d. Alligator
- e. Gila Monster
- f. King Snake
- g. Chuckawalla
- h. Diamondback Rattlesnake
- i. Racer Snake
- j. Copperhead
- k. Iguana

Page 32   Head of a Pit Viper

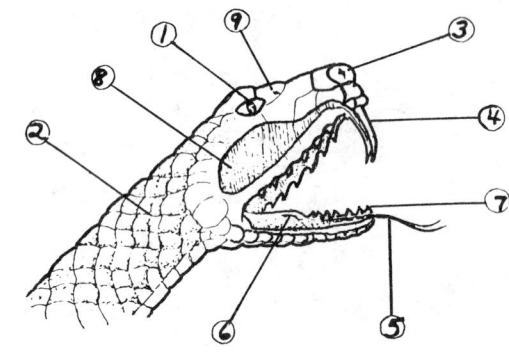

Page 34   Flyways of North America

ANSWER KEY

Page 38 What Is Your Outdoor I.Q.?
1. Bobcat, c
2. Grey Squirrel, e
3. Wolf, a
4. Beaver, d
5. Deer, b

Page 39
1. Bear, e
2. Skunk, c
3. Caribou, b
4. Fox, a
5. Rabbit, d

Page 41 Amoeba
1. Endoplasm
2. Food Vacuole
3. Ectoplasm
4. Nucleus
5. Contractile Vacuole
6. Membrane
7. Pseudopodia (False Foot)

Page 42 Euglena
1. Flagellum
2. Gullet
3. Eyespot
4. Contractile Vacuole
5. Nucleus
6. Pellicle
7. Chloroplasts
8. Contractile Fibers

Page 43 Paramecium
1. Cilia
2. Trichocyst
3. Food Vacuole
4. Oral Groove
5. Micronucleus
6. Gullet
7. Macronucleus
8. Food Vacuole Forming
9. Pellicle
10. Anal Pore
11. Contractile Vacuole

Page 44 Sponge
1. Osculum
2. Collar Cell
3. Pore
4. Spicule
5. Epidermal Cell

Page 45 Hydra
1. Mouth
2. Nematocyst
3. Ectoderm
4. Mesoglea
5. Endoderm
6. Bud
7. Base
8. Tentacle
9. Gastrovascular Cavity
10. Ovary

Page 46 Planaria
1. Eyespot
2. Brain
3. Intestine
4. Longitudinal Nerve
5. Transverse Nerve
6. Pharynx

Page 47 Earthworm—Digestive System
1. Mouth
2. Pharynx
3. Esophagus
4. Crop
5. Gizzard
6. Intestine
7. Anus

Page 48 Grasshopper—External
1. Ocelli Location (Simple Eye)
2. Compound Eye
3. Palp
4. Antenna
5. 1st Wings
6. 2nd Wings
7. Femur
8. Tibia
9. Tarsus
10. Ovipositor
11. Tynpanum (Eardrum)
12. Spiracle

Page 49 Grasshopper—Internal
1. Ovipositor
2. Anus
3. Abdominal Region
4. Heart
5. Egg Mass
6. Thoracic Region
7. Crop
8. Esophagus
9. Head Region
10. Antenna
11. Brain
12. Mouth
13. Palps
14. Salivary Gland
15. Ganglion and Nerve
16. Digestive Gland (Caecum)
17. Stomach
18. Malpighian Tubules
19. Intestine
20. Genital Opening

Page 50 Fish—External
1. Dorsal Fin
2. Eye
3. Nostril
4. Mouth
5. Operculum (Gill Cover)
6. Pectoral Fin
7. Lateral Line
8. Scale
9. Anal Fin
10. Caudal (Tail) Fin

Page 51 Fish—Internal
1. Dorsal Aorta
2. Kidney
3. Stomach
4. Ovary
5. Anus
6. Swim Bladder
7. Intestine
8. Liver
9. Heart

Page 52 Frog—Internal
1. Heart
2. Liver
3. Fat Body
4. Testis
5. Kidney
6. Bladder
7. Cloaca
8. Intestine
9. Pancreas
10. Stomach
11. Lung

Page 54 Branches of Science
1. m
2. a
3. p
4. o
5. c
6. t
7. h
8. b
9. s
10. r
11. l
12. j
13. k
14. q
15. d
16. n
17. g
18. f
19. i
20. e

ANSWER KEY

Page 59   Animal Records

1. Blue or Sulphur-Bottomed Whale
2. Giant Jellyfish
3. Giraffe
4. Tortoise
5. Spine-Tailed Swift (A Bird)
6. Whale Shark
7. Sperm Whale
8. Giant Squid
9. African Bush Elephant
10. Pygmy Shrew
11. Cheetah
12. Probably Man
13. Asiatic Elephant
14. American Opossum
15. Ostrich
16. Hummingbird
17. Marabou Stork
18. Gentoo Penguin
19. Anaconda
20. Sea Snakes (Hydro-phis belcheri)